COR FU

Travel with Marco Polo Insider Tips

INSIDER TIP
Your shortcut
to a great
experience

MARCO POLO
TOP HIGHLIGHTS

ESPLANADE ⭐
The ideal place to start your holiday. Order a cold espresso, listen to Corfiots debating on the next table, observe market sellers and hawkers selling their wares. In short, sit back and watch the world go by.

➤ p. 45, Corfu Town

ACHÍLLION ⭐
Built by Empress Elisabeth ("Sisi"), this dream castle was also a favourite haunt of Kaiser Wilhelm II of Germany.
📷 *Tip: Inside, only the staircase is photogenic. Outside, the statue of victorious Achilles is particularly impressive.*

➤ p. 57, Around Corfu

FALIRÁKI ⭐
Have a meal or a drink on the dockside with the water almost lapping at your feet. Then watch as the yachts sail by so close you can nearly touch them.
📷 *Tip: If you want to see the big cruise ships, you should make sure you are in position at around 6.15pm.*

➤ p. 44, Corfu Town

PALEÓ PERÍTHIA ⭐
Take a stroll through this idyllic, almost empty village. Don't worry though, its excellent tavernas are still open!
📷 *Tip: Do you like interesting shapes in your snaps? Then make sure you get a good angle on the S-shaped path from the village to its church.*

➤ p 73, The North

CAPE DRÁSTIS ⭐

Romantic painters were 'ere. The island's most striking cape with its beautiful white cliffs (see photo). Best seen from a boat.

📷 *Tip: To get the best photo, go to the end of the paved road, and then continue down the slope along the path across the fields for around 200m.*

➤ p. 71, The North

AFIÓNAS ⭐

A village to spend a day in. Narrow alleyways, beautiful old buildings, sensational views and – if you can brave the climb down – two glorious beaches.

📷 *Tip: To get the best photos of the village, walk along the short path from the church to the Anemos Taverna.*

➤ p. 75, The North

KASSIÓPI ⭐

An unbeatable coastal resort with a harbour, a fort, a pretty village square and beaches. If you still need convincing, there are great places to eat too!

➤ p. 62, The North

ÁGIOS GEÓRGIOS SOUTH ⭐

Are you the kind of person who loves soft sand and stunning dunes? Here you can watch the former being whipped up and forming the latter. For much the same reasons, this is also the perfect place to kite surf.

➤ p. 92, The South

ALONÁKI ⭐

Leave the world behind. Find a hotel on the sea's edge and then go and eat great Corfiot food in an idyllic garden.

➤ p. 93, The South

KAISER'S THRONE ⭐

Do not miss the spectacular sunsets in the hilly landscape around Pélekas.

➤ p. 107, Central Corfu

CONTENTS

THE NORTH

CENTRAL CORFU

CORFU TOWN (KÉRKYRA)

THE SOUTH

36   REGIONAL OVERVIEW

38   CORFU TOWN (KÉRKYRA)

Around Corfu Town   57

58   THE NORTH

Kassiópi   62
Around Kassiópi   65
Acharávi & Róda   66
Around Acharávi & Róda   70
Ágios Geórgios & Around   75
Paleokastrítsa   77
Around Paleokastrítsa   80

82   THE SOUTH

Ágios Górdis   86
Around Ágios Górdis   87
Messongí & Moraítika   88
Around Messongí & Moraítika   90
Ágios Geórgios South   92
Around Ágios Geórgios South   94

96   CENTRAL CORFU

Gouviá & Kontokáli   100
Dafníla & Dassiá   102
Around Dafníla & Dassiá   105
Pélekas, Glifáda & Mirtiótissa 107
Around Pélekas, Glifáda &
Mirtiótissa   110

CONTENTS

MARCO POLO TOP HIGHLIGHTS
2 Top 10 highlights

BEST OF CORFU
8 ... when it rains
9 ... on a budget
10 ... with children
11 ... classic experiences

GET TO KNOW CORFU
14 Discover Corfu
17 At a glance
18 Understand Corfu
22 True or false?

EATING, SHOPPING, SPORT
26 Eating & drinking
30 Shopping
32 Sport & activities

MARCO POLO REGIONS
36 Regional overview

DISCOVERY TOURS
112 Corfu at a glance
117 Ancient Kérkyra – a walking tour outside the old town
120 Villages and beaches around Pantokrátor
123 Shopping Corfu style – between Gouviá and Paleokastrítsa
125 Boat trip to Albania

GOOD TO KNOW
128 **HOLIDAY BASICS**
Arrival, Getting around, Emergencies, Essentials, Festivals & events, Weather

136 **USEFUL WORDS & PHRASES**
There's no need to be lost for words

138 **HOLIDAY VIBES**
Books, films, music and blogs

140 **TRAVEL PURSUIT**
The Marco Polo holiday quiz

142 **INDEX & CREDITS**

144 **DOS & DON'TS**
How to avoid slip-ups and blunders

⏱	Plan your visit	Eating/drinking	Rainy day activities
€–€€€	Price categories	Shopping	Budget activities
(*)	Premium-rate phone number	Going out	Family activities
		Top beaches	⚑ Classic experiences

(📖 A2) Refers to the removable pull-out map
(📖 a2) Refers to the inset street map on the pull-out map
(0) Located off the map

BEST OF CORFU

Kamináki Beach

BEST ☂

WHEN IT RAINS

ACTIVITIES TO BRIGHTEN YOUR DAY

JUST GO UNDER

➤ If you really want to get the better of the rain, just go under water. *Korfu Diving* offers scuba diving and snorkelling for rainy days. (photo)

➤ p. 34

JOURNEY BACK IN TIME

At the *Casa Parlante*, a group of friendly, young people takes you on a tour of this mansion once inhabited by a noble family 200 years ago. Today, this family has been recreated with animated wax figures, which introduce themselves, talk to you, offer a glass of liqueur and even serenade you. You can also take a look around the old kitchen at the end of the tour.

➤ p. 42, Corfu Town

KAMA SUTRA ON CORFU

Erotic images from the ancient Hindu Sanskrit text known as the Kama Sutra, or "verses of desire", were carved in stone to decorate Indian temples.

Three examples have made their way inside the *Old Palace* in Corfu Town.

➤ p. 47, Corfu Town

SHOPPING UNDER THE ARCADES

The *arcades of the main shopping streets* in the Old Town, especially Odós N. Theotóki, protect shoppers from the scorching heat and downpours. There are also a few cafés if you need some rest and refreshment.

➤ p .52, Corfu Town

JEWELLERY WITH A PERSONAL TOUCH

Shells that you find while walking along a beach can be transformed into lovely pieces of jewellery. Corfu's natural jewels can be cast in gold, silver or bronze at *Ílios Living Art* in Ágios Geórgios Pagón. Call to make an appointment. Casting normally takes two to four hours.

➤ p. 75, The North

BEST 🐷
ON A BUDGET
FOR SMALLER WALLETS

GOOD-VALUE GRUB
If you are looking for cheaper places to eat in Corfu Old Town, your best bet is to pick up some fast food. There is a range of Greek and international options where Viktoros Dousmani meets the Spianada, and in the area directly behind Hotel Konstantinoupolis on Zavitsianou Street.
➤ Corfu Town

HAPPY HOUR
Almost every bar on Corfu has a Happy Hour for cocktails and, in some places, other drinks are included too. Normally, the deal on offer is 2-for-1. However, be careful – in lots of places the offer is applied per person so each member of your party needs to order two drinks to take advantage of it.

LOOK AFTER THE PENNIES ...
AND PARTY
You don't need to flash much cash to go out in Corfu Town. Most of the clubs around the harbour don't charge entry and you can pick up cheap alcohol at the many off-licences and kiosks around them.
➤ Corfu Town

POOLS FOR ALL
You do not necessarily need to have booked a hotel with a pool to take advantage of a cooling dip. Many small hotels and apartment complexes also welcome guests who are not staying there. Just order something to eat or drink at the pool bar and then jump in free of charge.

SHARING IS CARING
It is very common, and not at all rude, to order a bottle of beer with two glasses on Corfu. And if you order one dish between two, waiters will nearly always bring a second plate and set of cutlery automatically. If you want to spread a big portion of food over several meals, ask for a doggy bag.

BEST

WITH CHILDREN

FUN FOR YOUNG AND OLD

HORSEPOWER

Colourful carriages course around Corfu's Old Town from morning until dusk. There is enough room in them for four adults (or two adults and four small children). The best time to take a ride is in the early evening.
➤ p.46, Corfu Town

EYEBALL THE PILOT

From the café terraces in Kanóni, you can see the whole airport beneath you. Up here you get a great view of the planes coming in at eye-level before they hit the runway below.
➤ p.49, Corfu Town

MINI DRIVERS

On almost every summer evening between 6pm and 10pm, there is a lively bustle at the southern end of the *Esplanade*. This is where a child's dream can become reality in the form of small electric cars that can be driven by anyone capable of holding a steering wheel and reaching the pedals.
➤ p.54, Corfu Town

LITTLE TRAIN TRIP

Tourist trains with a locomotive and three carriages are popular throughout Greece. They travel on rubber tyres and run on electric motors. The *trenáki* – little train – in Kérkyra sets off once an hour. Tours last 40 minutes.
➤ p.54, Corfu Town

CORFU DONKEY RESCUE

Just outside Paleokastrítsa, you can get up close and personal with some furry friends (photo). The sanctuary here has been rescuing donkeys from the Italian salami trade for many years, and welcomes visitors of all ages. You can stroke, brush and feed the animals, and even adopt your very own Eeyore. *Follow the signs from Doukades* | *corfu-donkey.com* | ⊞ *B8*
➤ The North

BEST

CLASSIC EXPERIENCES

ONLY ON CORFU

WORKING WITH OLIVE WOOD

Olive trees provide fruit and oil, as well as a unique wood that demands great skill from carvers. For decades, Thomás has been one of the best and has devoted himself to this craft in his studio *By Tom* in Corfu's Old Town.
➤ p. 53, Corfu Town

LITTLE ORANGES

The bitter fruit of the *kumquat tree* has become a new trademark of the island. Try it for yourself! Liqueurs, jams, sweets and many other goodies can be found in the shop run by the Vassilákis family in Corfu Town or its sales room at Achíllion (photo).
➤ p. 53 and p. 57, Corfu Town

HIGH-KICK LIKE IN HOLLYWOOD

Dance like Zorba the Greek! Thanks to the blockbuster film of the same name, the *syrtáki* has become synonymous with Greek dancing. You can delight in watching professional dancers perform on the terrace at the *Golden Beach* bar, and even give it a try yourself!
➤ p. 89, The South

FISH IN THE GARDEN OF EDEN

Corfiots love lush gardens, and they also love fish soup called *bourdétto* made with scorpion fish. In the *Alonáki* Taverna near Chalikúnas you can enjoy the best of both – a version of the traditional dish made to a particularly tasty recipe, served in beautiful surroundings.
➤ p. 93, The South

WATCH OUT!

The Corfiots celebrate *Easter* in their own special way. On Easter Saturday, hundreds of clay water jugs are thrown out of windows and from balconies onto the streets in the Old Town. Thousands of cheerful spectators watch this wet spectacle that follows the magnificent Easter procession.
➤ p. 131, Corfu Town

GET TO KNOW CORFU

Melons for sale! Kassiópi

DISCOVER CORFU

Empress Sisi built it as a holiday home, Kaiser Wilhelm II loved it: Villa Achíllion

Fasten your seat belts, please! Leaving the coast of Italy behind you, your pilot will start his descent where the Adriatic merges into the Ionian Sea. You will be greeted by the sight of other Greek island outcrops before Corfu comes into view.

EAGLE-EYED

The beaches! Even from a height of 4,000m / 13,000ft, you can see narrow strips of sand hugging the many coves along the rugged coastline, while wide open bays are fringed with broad sandy beaches against a backdrop of green. Your plane descends lower, brushing over a sea of olive trees interspersed with prickly cypresses. Scattered among the hills are dreamy villages dating back centuries.

734 BCE
Foundation of Corfu Town

229 BCE
Corfu submits to the rule of Rome

395-1204
Byzantine period

1386
The Venetians take over Corfu

1453
The Ottoman Empire takes over all of Greece – with the exception of the Ionian Islands

1797
Napoleon occupies Corfu

1815
Corfu becomes a British protectorate

Above Lefkími in the island's south, the plane begins its final descent. Green hills shoot by on your left, while on your right crowds of people are waving from "Mouse Island". At this point you might feel a rush of adrenaline or break into a nervous sweat as it appears the plane is about to nose-dive into the sea. Don't worry though: the cockpit crew expertly land it on the runway that was built in a lagoon. Congratulations, you've arrived on Corfu to start your adventure.

THE ADVENTURE BEGINS

It's time to explore Greece's sixth largest island. The island's 112,000 inhabitants are also waiting to greet and get to know you. Most Corfiots speak good English as well as some German and Italian. This is mainly attributed to the island's history: under Venetian rule for over 400 years, Corfu was then conquered by Napoleon and the French followed by the British. Unification with Greece was only concluded in 1864, after Greece had become independent from the Turks. Corfu was never under Turkish rule, which means the island has absorbed far less oriental influence than some other Greek islands and mainland regions.

CHARMING TOWN

Your first port of call should be Corfu Town. Known to the Greeks as Kérkyra, Corfu Town is a vibrant place stretching several kilometres directly along the coast. Sailing yachts, fishing boats, ferries and cruise ships sail past, almost within

1864
Corfu becomes part of independent Greece

1941–1944
Italian and German occupation

1967–1974
Military dictatorship followed by democracy

2002
The euro replaces the drachma

2010–2018
Greece narrowly avoids national bankruptcy through strict economic measures and financial aid

2020
Greece continues to experience instability

reach. Land is visible in every direction, from the island's highest mountain (over 900m / 2,953ft) in the north to the mountain massifs of northwest Greece and Albania on the mainland, which are usually covered in snow between November and April. The view alone would be reason enough to visit in winter when the Corfiots are mainly left to their own devices.

It is worth visiting the island's capital more than once. Excursion boats offer trips to Corfu Town from many resorts along the east coast. In the morning you can go shopping – no department stores for a change, but hundreds of small shops along crooked Old Town lanes and under shady arcades, where the owners themselves stand behind the counter. At the weekly market, you'll see fish you only know from the aquarium. Watch the hustle and bustle while you enjoy an espresso or a *freddo cappuccino*. After lunch, you could chill out at the Beach Club, right next to an old Venetian fort.

BEACHES TO DIE FOR

The island is surrounded by beaches, and there is such a great variety that every-body can find that perfect dream beach. Those on the east coast facing the mainland, where most of the large seaside hotels are located, are mostly of shin-gles or smooth pebbles, often several hundred metres long but always fairly narrow. Many of the hotels directly on the beach offset this by providing lush, green lawns around a pool, while tavernas place deckchairs in their flowery gardens and hang hammocks between the trees. Wooden jetties jut out into the protected bays of the straits. This is where the sun worshippers lie, before climbing down ladders into the water. Some beaches are used as water-sport centres.

The east coast is perfect for waterskiing, paragliding and paddle boats – how-ever, surfers will be rather disappointed. The north coast is better suited for those who like long, wide beaches. The tavernas and lounge bars are the perfect places for a break and some refreshments during long strolls along the beach.

Corfu's west coast facing the open sea offers the greatest variety of beaches. They begin at Cape Drástis in the far northwest, where the brave climb into the water from white rocks and, if the sea is completely calm, swim out along the white sandstone cliffs. The golden crescents of sand in the bays of Ágios Stéfanos and Ágios Geórgios Pagón are miles long, while most of the 20-plus beaches on the fragmented Paleokastrítsa Bay are hidden away among the steep cliffs.

INSIDER TIP
Only reached by boat

Some large hotels have opened on the few beaches in the middle of the west coast: in Glifáda, Pélekas and Ágios Górdis. It then becomes more secluded again. The beach at the northern spit between the sea and Lake Chalikúnas is almost completely deserted, and the few bathers to the southwest of the lake lose them-selves in the expansive, Sahara-like dunes of Ágios Geórgios Argirádon. In the extreme south, a noisy counterpoint is provided by Kávos with its narrow strips of sand, where there is an all-day party and plenty of close contact on the beach.

AT A GLANCE

100,854
Population

Lincoln: 100,160

4 MILLION

Olive trees
(approximately)

217km / 135 miles
Coastline

Anglesey: 200km / 124 miles

585km² / 226 sq miles
Area

Islay: 620km² / 240 sq miles

HIGHEST POINT: PANTOKRÁTOR

911m / 3,000 ft

A road leads to the summit

WARMEST MONTH

JULY
31.1°C

WETTEST MONTHS

NOV
DEC

62 BUS SERVICES
connect the town with the villages

KÉRKYRA

is the name of Corfu town
and island in Greek

2km / 1.25 miles

separate Corfu from Albania

UNDERSTAND CORFU

FROM TOURIST TO RESIDENT

After a holiday on Corfu, many people dream of settling permanently on the island. Thousands of Brits live here alongside expats of many other nationalities. Foreigners are welcomed for their contribution to the local economy, but it can be hard for non-Greeks to set up their own businesses, and those that manage it are likely to be subject to regular official inspections. In-comers who are really innovative and whose business ventures don't compete with the locals have the best chance of being accepted. One good example of a family who has succeeded is the Kalkmanns in Afiónas. They buy olive oil from regional farmers and sell it in attractive packaging – a win-win situation for both parties.

BANKS & BUILDING BOOM

Before the country was declared bankrupt in 2010, many Greeks were living in a land of milk and honey. Their banks would call regularly trying to sell them a loan. "What, only 20,000 euros? No chance, take 50,000," the banks would say, knowing full well who owned what land and how much money their clients earned. New building developments were then proposed, making people believe they had sufficient financial means to invest. Many people unfortunately succumbed to temptation: you'll notice that the roads are full of now-ageing luxury limousines, SUVs and off-roaders, and that there are many unfinished buildings. The banks' generosity stopped as soon as the financial crisis hit. The Greeks are now in serious debt. The only upside is that the banks now struggle to find buyers for houses they want to put up for auction.

HOISTING THE FLAG

Most Corfiots are obsessed with flags. Two flags in particular are held in high regard. The white and blue flag stands for the Greek nation. The second flag depicts a black Byzantine double eagle on a yellow background. This is the flag of the Greek Orthodox Church and is most often seen outside churches and monasteries on the island.

Many football fans also like to wave the flags of their favourite teams: red and white are the colours of Olympiakos Piraeus, a famous Greek team from the port of Athens that counts many Corfiots among its supporters. You'll see the number 7 is painted on many house facades, street walls and traffic signs around Corfu; it stands for gate no. 7 to the stadium in Piraeus, where only the most dedicated (and wildest) fans congregate. The main rival team from Athens, Panathinaikós, is represented by the number 13.

UNLUCKY ROYALS

Corfu was once a paradise for European royal families. Sisi, the

Empress of Austria, and Wilhelm II, the German Kaiser, both owned a small castle here, while the Palaia Anaktora housed the Kings of Greece. Prince Philip, the late husband of Queen Elizabeth II, was even born on the island. However, few of these royals enjoyed a happy end: Sisi was assassinated, while Wilhelm was forced to abdicate. Constantine II, the last monarch of Greece, had to pay off tax debts by selling his palace on Corfu. Philip's mother suffered from schizophrenia, but Philip himself went on to become the consort of Queen Elizabeth II.

CORFU PHILHARMONICS

Forget the blasting sounds from the island's beach clubs; Corfu has a more illustrious musical tradition. Every larger town has its own philharmonic society, which offers music lessons for children either for free or at an affordable cost. You can often hear them practising when you walk by. The young players often participate in marching bands and other public parades, so if you're lucky you might get the opportunity to see the full effect of this musical philanthropy. Some of the philharmonic orchestras take part in international guest performances.

Admittedly, classical music is not to everyone's taste. Guitars often hang in tavernas for guests to play. The traditional, almost Neapolitan-sounding *kantádes* can still sometimes be heard on the island, while a more popular sound is the traditional *rembétiko*. These protest songs, dating from the 1920s and 1930s, have seen a revival since the financial crisis, with contemporary reinterpretations. *Rembétika* are also played in discos and clubs

The blue and white Greek national flag flutters beside the yellow and black Greek Orthodox Church flag

God's ambassadors on Earth – icons can be seen and are honoured all over Corfu

along with hits from the Scorpions or other heavy metal bands.

The island is also the birthplace of two Eurovision Song Contest performers: Vicky Leandros, who represented Luxembourg in 1972, and the more famous Sakis Rouvas, who successfully performed for Greece in 2004 and 2009 with "Shake It", Greece's best-selling song.

GAMBLING FEVER

Corfiots are crazy about sport. Even in rural villages, a football or basketball game is always showing on one of the flat screens in the *kafenía* and bars. This obsession with sport has little to do with athletic prowess or enthusiasm: the state-owned OPAP bookmakers have thousands of agencies throughout Greece, and are largely responsible for the Greeks' love of gambling. You will also encounter people wandering the streets selling tickets and scratch cards for the three major national lottery companies. Greek Olympic champions sometimes receive a betting office licence to enable them to secure some real gold.

MULTICULTURAL

Globalisation has not overlooked this small island. Foreigners have always played an important role in determining Corfu's destiny, formerly as rulers, but now more often as either tourists or workers. The olive harvest would be impossible without day labourers from Albania, and there would be fewer fish on the menu without the help of Egyptian fishermen. Many houses would remain unbuilt and many hotel rooms uncleaned without Bulgarian and Romanian muscle power. Even the evening entertainment would be less interesting without multilingual staff from the Czech Republic and Hungary, who are employed by many hotels and beach bars.

GOOD COMPANY

Corfiots do not like spending time on their own. Even a cosy twosome is reserved for a certain hour of the day. At other times, Greeks prefer the company of a *paréa* – a group of friends or acquaintances, who regularly meet up to drink coffee or eat, or go to the disco or on holiday together. The question asked by others after a night out or a trip away is not what the hotel or food was like but how the *paréa* was.

In case you do have to go it alone, you will always be accompanied by the island's saints. They are present as icons wherever you go on the island – whether in the car, in the ticket booth or in the fields – either as printed images or painted on church and chapel walls and hanging on the sides of the road. You know you are always in safe hands and in good company.

CRISIS? WHAT CRISIS?

For many Corfiots, the Greek financial crisis that erupted in 2010 has turned into a chronic, untreatable illness. Salaries, pensions and social benefits have all been cut, while taxes have risen considerably. Unemployment remains very high, particularly among the young – and there are no real signs

MY FAMILY AND OTHER ANIMALS

First broadcast in 2016, *The Durrells* is a TV comedy drama set on Corfu that has attracted crowds of new tourists to the island. The series is based on the famous Durrell family: Lawrence was a successful novelist, while his younger brother Gerald founded Jersey zoo and was a writer, broadcaster and naturalist for the BBC. The brothers spent some of their youth with their eccentric mother on Corfu, and Gerald wrote about his experiences in the highly entertaining book *My Family and Other Animals,* which offers an amusing insight into the fauna of the island. Corfu may not be the first destination on your mind when you think of an island safari, but the island's flamingos are a spectacular sight. They migrate to the salt lake at Lefkími between October and May and can be spotted standing majestically on one leg – the typical posture for these pink-feathered birds.

of recovery. The Corfiots have adapted their lifestyle accordingly. They plant vegetables instead of ornamental shrubs, only order what they can eat in tavernas, buy smaller cars and have stopped building new houses. They also give each other a helping hand whenever they can. As long as the tourists keep coming, the island's economy will survive.

TRUE OR FALSE?

EVERYONE DANCES THE SYRTÁKI

Ever since Anthony Quinn danced it in the cult classic *Zorba the Greek*, the rest of the world has assumed that the *syrtáki* is the definition of traditional Greek dance. Little do they know that the dance was in fact invented specially for the film because it was assumed that authentic Greek dancing would be too complicated for an American audience. As a result, the best place to see this dance is in the kind of bars and tavernas from which Greeks generally keep their distance. The only exception to this is the occasional nightclub where a few young Greeks may show off their *syrtáki* skills in the hope of impressing some foreign visitors.

GREECE RELIES ON BAIL-OUTS

Post-pandemic, the financial crisis in Greece may seem very long ago, but nonetheless don't be tempted to tell Greeks that their economy was saved by taxpayers in far-off countries. Most people here did not see much evidence of foreign help – the money very often went straight back out of the country to settle interest payments for Greece's debt. There are however two sides to every story, and no-one knows how bad things could have got if no money had come in from the rest of the world.

LAND OF CONFUSION

Corfiots are quite relaxed where spelling is concerned, a custom that can confuse many a tourist. In Greek, place names can be written differently on signs and maps, while the Latin spelling is even more haphazard. "Agios" meaning "Saint" is a good example; it is sometimes written as "Agios" (as in the Marco Polo guides) or "Aghios" or even "Ayios". All three spellings are accepted and combined as the Greeks please.

But that's not all – things get even more confusing on entering villages. Although most places use house numbers, they are rarely marked on buildings, and even the village locals don't know them. Some visitors may like this laid-back approach, but it can be frustrating when you're trying to locate a particular address. Your best bet is usually to ask around.

A RUBBISH PROBLEM

Corfu has a real problem keeping a lid on its rubbish. Towns and villages are clean and tidy, but the main roads at their edge often become makeshift tips, with rubbish piled up along them. Refuse collection only removes the contents of official bins, so the stacks of binbags and cardboard boxes outside them are often left the whole summer long ... and it does not take long for them to stink to high heaven. This does not stop locals piling old mattresses, fridges and other scrap on top. Even simple solutions to the problem, like crushing drink cans are greeted with an unhealthy dose of Corfiot scepticism. Every autumn,

Dappled sunlight in one of the island's olive groves

the local government promises to find solutions to the issue. And for regular visitors, it adds a (usually dashed) element of excitement to a trip each year to see if they have been successful.

ORGANIC FARMERS AND OLIVE GROVES

There are many farmers on Corfu who would like to produce organic goods which often have better prospects for sales and can command higher prices – especially for wine and olive oil. However, the hurdles are too high as it is difficult for them to keep their crops a sufficient distance from the sprayed fields of "chemical farmers". As a result, there is still no press on the island that exclusively processes organically grown olives. Despite no eco labelling, you can be sure the oil is of a good and healthy quality, as extensive insecticide spraying from the air has been stopped. Each farmer can decide whether to use chemicals or rely on a natural fertilizer using manure placed in bags under trees to gently drain the rainwater into the soil.

PLANNING – WHAT'S THAT?!

Do you know what tomorrow will bring? Do as the Corfiots do and don't waste your time planning for the long term. Large events and festivals are only made public a few days in advance, while timetables or the opening times of museums or excavation sites are posted online at short notice. Vague arrangements to meet the following morning, afternoon, evening or even next week are made, adding the all-important "*ta leme*" – "we'll talk again later." You can then expect a call one hour beforehand to confirm the exact time – give or take the customary half hour.

EATING
SHOPPING
SPORT

Restaurants in Kérkyra's Old Town

EATING & DRINKING

Corfiots would prefer to stay at home rather than eat alone or just as a couple. A meal can only be fully enjoyed with the right *paréa*, the simple Greek word meaning a group of family or friends gathering together to enjoy each other's company. It can take some time to round up all the guests, which is one reason why most Greeks rarely eat before 9pm.

IT'S ALL ABOUT THE *PARÉA*

Eating in a *paréa* is one way to get a sense of what kind of form a chef is in. Nobody orders food just for themselves, and certainly not before quizzing the waiter about what is on today's menu. There is not a set sequence of menu courses as we know it – waiters serve dishes to the table as soon as they are ready in the kitchen and you will only find written menus in touristy restaurants. Greeks eat *mezedákia*, a wide variety of specialities on as many plates as possible.

Most waiters are casually dressed, and they start by covering the linen tablecloth with a paper one; children are invited to scribble on it and nobody feels the need to hide the first food stains under a napkin. A medium-sized plate is placed for each guest; cutlery and serviettes are taken from the obligatory bread basket, and guests help themselves to water, wine or beer. A toast is then made to the good company round the table with *"jámas"* meaning "to our health".

The waiter places all the dishes in the middle of the table. Everybody takes what – and as much as they want. Fish and meat are usually served on large platters and everyone helps themselves. All the plates, even the empty ones, are left on the table. The waiters don't take any away so that the *paréa* can see how well they dined.

Greek salad (left) and baklava (right)

ON THE HOUSE

Desserts are brought out with the bill (which is paid by one person) and are often served on the house with a round of *tsípouro*, a good-quality brandy similar to the Italian grappa. Where's the Oúzo? you might ask. On Corfu, oúzo is rarely drunk after the meal; it is usually enjoyed as an aperitif or during the meal. Once you have been given your change, a tip can be left on the table on leaving the restaurant.

NOT THE ONLY WAY

Don't worry if you are not invited to join a *paréa*, you won't starve. Lone diners and couples are welcomed everywhere and at most times of the day and night. Nearly all restaurants and tavernas that don't survive solely from tourism serve warm meals throughout the day, from a proper English breakfast first thing in the morning until midnight. Only occasionally do some restaurants close between 4pm and 6pm. You are also not restricted to traditional Greek pubs known as *mezedopolío, tsipourádiko or ouzerí*. The city and holiday resorts have a wide selection of restaurants serving international cuisine, from pizzerias and souvlaki grills to Indian, Chinese and Italian. There are even English pubs serving traditional pub grub.

If you are after a quick bite, snack bars known as *psistariá* are a good alternative to restaurants. Standing up or sitting down, you can order chicken or pork *gýros* in pita bread or on a plate *(mérida)*, meatballs, local sausage and – quite often – chicken. Chips on the side are omnipresent.

Those with a sweet tooth will make their way to the *zácharoplastío*, the

INSIDER TIP
Need a little something

A good Greek coffee wakes the senses

Greek pastry shop, with its mainly eastern Mediterranean specialities such as *baklavás* and *kataífi* ("angel's hair"), along with cream and sponge cakes.

QUENCHING YOUR THIRST

Water will always be brought to the table with every meal, and in villages this can be good-quality tap water or even fresh spring water. Wine from the barrel is available everywhere, and many restaurant owners are proud of their extensive wine menus with a wide selection of Greek bottled wines. *Retsína*, the white wine flavoured with resin, is not very popular on Corfu. The famous aniseed schnapps, *oúzo*, competes with the subtle *tsípouro* to be the favourite tipple among locals.

The Corfiot speciality, *tzitzimbírra*, is a non-alcoholic drink made of lemon juice, sugar, water and a touch of ginger. You can sample this from the beginning of May in inland villages such as Sokráki in the north of the island. It almost disappeared in the early 1990s, but the demand created by holidaymakers led to the traditional drink remaining on the market. If you order it, you are helping to preserve a tradition – and it is very tasty indeed.

THE COMPLEXITIES OF COFFEE

The Greeks drink coffee at any time of the day. However, ordering it in Greece is something of a science. You have the choice between a small cup of Greek coffee, *kafé ellenikó*; hot instant coffee, usually called *ness sestó*; cold, whipped instant coffee served with ice cubes, *frappé*; and the trendy *freddo* as either cappuccino or espresso. If you order Greek coffee, you must always say how sweet you want it because the ground coffee is mixed with sugar and then brewed: *skétto* is without, *métrio* with a little and *glikó* with a lot of sugar. And, of course, Greek coffee is always without milk. If you want to have your hot or cold Nescafé with milk you just have to add *"mä gala"*. On Corfu, the older people like to put a small shot of oúzo in their coffee and order *"kafé ellinikó mä polí lígo úso mässa"*.

Today's Recommendations

Starters

FAVA
A paste made from yellow split peas, onions and olive oil

NOUBOÚLO
Lightly smoked ham

TARAMÁ
Fish roe paste – red or white

Fish

BAKALJÁROS ME SKORDALJÁ
White fish – normally cod – served with a potato-garlic puree

BOURDÉTTO
Corfiot fish dish traditionally made with scorpion fish (skate is also common) in a tangy tomato broth

GALÉO ME SKORDALIÁ
Boneless dogfish fillets with a garlicky potato dip

MARÍDES
Crisp, fried anchovies, eaten whole

Meat

BEKRI MEZÉ
Mildly spicy pork and red wine stew

JUVÉTSI
Pasta bake with beef (occasionally, with lamb)

PASTITSÁDA
Beef and chicken with pasta

SOFRÍTO
Beef, marinated in garlic and vinegar and braised in wine

Salad

CHORIÁTIKI
Mixed salad with feta and olives

CHÓRTA
Salad made with boiled chard or foraged greens

PATSÁRIA
Beetroot salad, often served with its leaves

SHOPPING

Small shopkeepers have successfully survived the onslaught of supermarkets on the island. Only food retailers are feeling the pressure from big-name discounters, and the traditional one-euro shops are suffering from the large number of Chinese bric-a-brac shops with red lanterns in front.

Shopping on Corfu will not blow your holiday budget. On the whole, the selection of stores is staid and conventional and lacks a wow factor. Shoes are the only items to follow the latest fashion trends. Most of the arts and crafts for sale are made in Greece and Corfu, with some Greek art also available to buy. And Corfu's plethora of culinary specialities will spoil any well-intentioned diet plans.

HONEY, KUMQUATS, ETC

If you have a sweet tooth, you will find it hard not to fall in love with Corfiot honey, which can be made into delicious, high-energy (for the exercise mad) sesame bars. Kumquats, or *koum kouáts* in Greek – little oranges, a maximum of 4cm / 1.5 inches long, with a yellowy-orange skin – are a unique island speciality. The vitamin-rich citrus fruit is made into marmalade and liquor or sold as candied fruit. The latest trend is a newly-created eau de toilette with a fruity, tangy kumquat aroma.

ARTS & CRAFTS

Objects carved out of olive wood are really special: bowls, cups, salad servers, as well as small pieces of furniture, such as stools and tables. You can find them in several shops in the Old Town of Corfu and in mountain villages, including Makrádes, Lákones and Strinílas, as well as the beach resort Acharávi. The best place to buy coloured glassware made on Corfu for

Driftwood sailing boats (left), souvenir stall (right)

your home is in Ágios Stéfanos Avliotón or in the Old Town of Corfu, where there are also several antique shops.

Driftwood items are currently in trend, such as decorative ships with sails made of faded jeans. Corfiot pottery is always a favourite among tourists, whether for decorative or household use.

MUSIC
Many souvenir shops sell CDs with Greek music à la Alexis Zorba at reasonable prices – although no Greek would ever buy them. If you are looking for good recordings of up-to-date Greek music of any kind, you should visit the special shops in the island's capital where you will get good advice and be able to listen to the music.

OLIVE OIL
Pure olive oil from Corfu tastes even better if you know which grove it has come from. However, the security standards now in force when you are flying mean that you should only buy it in cans. Another delicious Corfiot speciality is olive paste.

INSIDER TIP
Great as a dip or spread

WINE, LIQUEURS & SPIRITS
Corfiot wine is not a star of the global wine trade, but is a delicious element of any visit to the island. If you do decide to support a local winemaker who has a stall at the side of the road, make sure you drink the wine immediately. Even a few hours on a flight home can turn these coarse wines into harsh vinegar.

OPENING HOURS
Shops are usually open from 8.30am to 2pm from Monday to Saturday, and again from 6pm to 9pm on Tuesday, Thursday and Friday. Most supermarkets and souvenir shops are open from 8.30am to 11pm.

SPORT & ACTIVITIES

Corfu is no training camp location for high-performance athletes. The island takes a slower pace in terms of the sporting activities available, whether on, above or under water, on horseback, on foot or on a mountain bike.

Yoga and meditative courses are also available for those who prefer to slow things right down on holiday. But if you feel the need for more speed, you can take the helm of your own boat with up to 30 horsepower (HP) without even having a sailing licence.

BOAT TRIPS & CRUISES

You can take a short cruise lasting one or several days around Corfu on a variety of boats. *Corfu Yachting (tel. 26 61 09 94 70| corfuyachting.com)* in the marina at Gouviá offers the greatest range of tours.

A one-day cruise on a wooden schooner dating from 1960 costs 100 euros per person, and 80 euros on a sailing catamaran. Glass-bottomed boats and traditional *káikis* are also available. If you want real luxury, you can hire a sleek motor yacht – complete with captain – for six people for a hefty 3,950 euros for 24 hours (drinks included).

After just a brief explanation, you can set off in your rented motorboat (up to 30HP) without even having a licence. The hire company will tell you exactly where you are allowed to go. All boats are equipped with life jackets and a two-way radio. There are boat-hire companies with the usual facilities in many resorts on the east and north coasts, as well as on the small neighbouring island of Páxos.

DIVING

Around Corfu you'll find a rich submarine life. There are very few restrictions on diving, making the area ideal for

Sailing round Corfu

this sport. The best diving grounds are on the coast between Paleokastrítsa and Érmones. As this rocky area can only be reached from the land at a few places, most of the dives start from boats. All diving centres on Corfu give individual instruction and organise dives for tourists; and offer lessons for beginners, special courses and one-to-one scuba diving instruction for individual divers. Absolute beginners can take introductory diving courses (44 euros) and snorkelling tours (30 euros). 🐢 *Korfu Diving (Paleokastrítsa | Ambeláki Bay | tel. 26 6304 16 04 | korfudiving.com) and Corfu Dive Club (Liápades | Hotel Blue Princess | mobile tel. 69 77 59 75 88 | corfudiveclubub.com)*

GOLF

Corfu has the greenest and most-cared-for 18-hole golf course in Greece. The high trees and small ponds give the course in the Ropa Valley its special appeal; the club-house, with its restaurant and small pro-shop, is another plus. Guests are welcome. *Corfu Golf Club (tel. 26 61 09 42 20; in winter, tel. 21 06 92 30 28 | corfugolfclub.com)*

HIKING

With its many shady paths, green valleys and countless villages, Corfu is an ideal hiking region. You can never get completely lost because there is almost always a village in sight. There are, however, few well-marked trails and no good guide books or maps to walking on the island. Independent hiking can, therefore, be a risky game. As a result, it makes sense to book a guide if you want to explore the island on foot. The

INSIDER TIP
Don't risk getting lost

best walks on the island are on the (poorly marked) *Corfu Trail*, a path that

Those looking for a challenge should follow the Corfu Trail right across the island

runs for 138 miles / 222km from Cape Akotíri Arkoúdia in the south to Cape Akotíri Ágias Ekaterínis in the north. For more information and links to hike organisers along this long-distance path, visit *thecorfutrail.com*.

HORSE RIDING

The best-run riding stable on the island – with tours on offer for beginners and experts – is *Trailriders (Mon–Sat 10am–noon and 5–7pm | free transfers in the region between Paleokastrítsa and Gouviá | near Áno Korakiána, signposted from there | tel. 69 46 65 33 17 | trailriderscorfu.com)*.

MOUNTAIN BIKING

Three companies offer guided mountain bike tours with various levels of difficulty. They, and some other smaller firms, also have bikes for hire. Guided day tours start at 35 euros (10% internet discount). The best mountain-bike specialists are: *The Corfu Mountainbike Shop (Dassiá | on the main road | tel. 26 61 09 33 44 | mountainbikecorfu.gr); S-A-F Travel/ Hellas Bike (Skombú | on the Gouviá- Paleokastrítsa road | tel. 26 61 09 75 58 | mobile tel. 69 45 52 80 31); S-Bikes (on the main road | Acharávi | tel. 26 63 06 41 15 | corfumountainbikes. com); Ionian Bike (Ágios Ioánnis | mobile tel. 69 09 75 98 17 | ionianbike-hike.nl)*.

TENNIS

Most of the large hotels have tennis courts, some of which are open to people not staying in the hotel. The best complex that is open all year round and very popular with Corfiots has seven floodlit courts under the shade of pine trees: *Dafníla Tennis Club (near Grecotel Dafníla Bay in Daphníla | tel. 26 61 09 05 70)*.

WATERSPORTS & SAILING

There are watersports centres at all of the main hotels and popular beaches.

The bays between Dassiá and Kontokáli are particularly suited to water-skiing: short rentals cost about 25 euros. There are also plenty of other fun options e.g. banana-boat (15 euros/ride). Paragliding is also available on many beaches – there can be significant price differences depending on the season and centre. A solo glider pays between 45 and 50 euros; tandems, from 60 to 70 euros.

Windsurfers, dinghy and catamaran sailors are drawn to the west coast where the winds are stronger. There are good centres in Paleokastrítsa, Ágios Geórgios Pagón and Érmones. Kite-surfing is only possible in Ágios Geórgios Argirádon. Standup paddleboards are available for hire and guided paddleboard tours are also organised by *kite-club-corfu.com.*

Those with a licence for open-sea sailing can rent yachts by the week – some with a skipper. *Corfu Yachting (Marina Gouviá | tel. 26 61 09 94 70 | corfuyachting.com); Tsigorítis Maritime Holidays (Marina Gouviá | tel. 26 61 09 18 88 | tsirigotis.com).*

If there's no wind, use the windsurf board as a paddle board instead

REGIONAL OVERVIEW

Rugged cliffs, long beaches and a mountain peak

Roda

Kassi

THE NORTH p.58

Ag. Geórgios

Paleokastrítsa

Gouviá

CENTRAL CORFU p.96

Kanali

Pélekas

Easy-to-reach resorts, attractive hillsides, verdant bays

Ág. Gord

Dunes, sand, windsurfing, olive groves and a large lake

I o n i o   P e l a g o s

5 km
3.11 mi

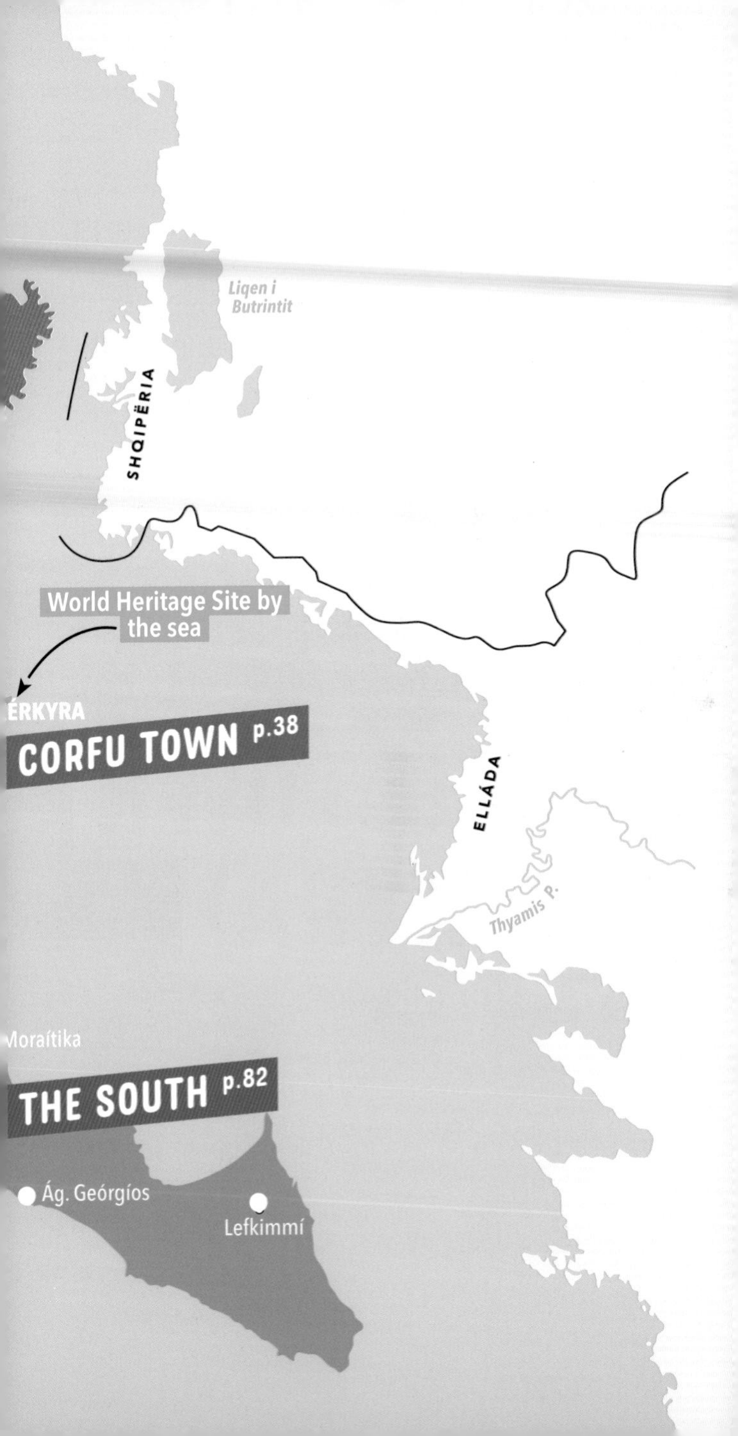

Liqen i
Butrintit

SHQIPËRIA

World Heritage Site by
the sea

ÉRKYRA

CORFU TOWN p.38

ELLÁDA

Thyamis P.

Moraítika

THE SOUTH p.82

● Ág. Geórgios   ● Lefkimmí

CORFU TOWN (KÉRKYRA)

UNIQUELY BEAUTIFUL

No matter where you are based on the island, it's worth visiting the town of Corfu at least three times. You need a morning to stroll through the market and shopping district and to visit the museums, churches and forts, followed by a spot of shopping and eating. Finish your first day chilling out by the sea at one of the many beach bars.

For your second visit to the city, return in the late afternoon to wander along the Esplanade, try one of the many types of coffee under

View over Kérkyra

the shady arcades, take a horse-drawn carriage ride through the Old Town and enjoy a sundowner while watching the sunset over the Corfu skyline. Meet the locals for an evening meal before immersing yourself in Greek nightlife. The choice of music is entirely up to you. This second trip will probably leave you hungry to see even more on an inevitable third trip. This time, take a cheap city bus up to the little palaces, Mon Repos and Achíllion, or to Kanóni, where the views out to two little islands make it Corfu's most popular spot for photos.

CORFU TOWN (KÉRKYRA)

Ethnikís Antistáseos — Εθνικής Αντιστάσεως

Neo Limáni

Yard Club

54 Dreamy Nights

Kérkyra - Palaiokastrítsa — Κέρκυρα - Παλαιοκαστρίτσα

Στρ. Ξενοφώντος

Σπύρου Μουργη / Napoléontos

Σπυρίδων Βασιλείου

Ποταμού

Αλ. Παναγούλη

Μιλτ

Ρήγα Φεραίου

MARCO POLO HIGHLIGHTS

★ **FALIRÁKI**
A relaxed spot to eat on the waterfront
➤ p. 44

★ **BYZANTINE MUSEUM**
Icons with great stories to tell exhibited
in an old church building ➤ p. 45

★ **ESPLANADE**
A beautiful open space with many
pavement cafés ➤ p. 45

★ **ARCHAEOLOGICAL MUSEUM**
Masterpieces of early Greek art ➤ p. 47

★ **MON REPOS**
A small castle in an overgrown park
➤ p. 48

★ **CAVALIERI ROOF GARDEN**
An evening spent above the roofs of the
town ➤ p. 55

★ **IMABÁRI**
The city's nicest beach bar, day and night
➤ p. 55

★ **ACHÍLLION**
German-Austrian fairy-tale castle
➤ p. 57

Κέρκυρα - Αλεπού

Αγ. σταείου Κατα. μίδη
Λευκάδος
Κεφαλληνίας
Παξών
Επτανήσου

Κέρκυρα - Γύρος Αχιλλείου

Achíllion ★

18 Vídos

400 m
437 yd

Ionio Pelagos

Káthe Práma Ston Kairó Tou
Ágios Spiridonas Church
Byzantine Museum ★
7
Velvet
Bellissimo
Blanc du Nil
Arseniou
6 Faliráki (Ágios Nikólas Gate) ★
Vassilákis
Imabári ★
Gyros Souvláki Grill House
10
Synagogue
Museum of Asian Art
Faliráki Beach
New Fortress
5
Polytéchno
Lalaoúnis
(Néo Froúrio)
Graal
3
Tabernita
By Tom
Mexicana
Pérgola
2
Aegli
Cambiéllo
4
Weekly
8
market
9 Esplanade ★
1 Old Fortress
Markora
11 Kípos tou Laoú
Old Fortress Café
Patoúnis
Roúvas
Soúsi
O Kritikós
Ektós Skédio
Casa Parlante
Fairymade
Cavalieri Roof Garden ★

British Cemetery 13
12 Archaeological Museum ★

Ormos Garitsas

Agías Efthímias Convent 15
Mon Repos beach

Palaiópolis basilica 14

Kanóni, Vlachérna Monastery 17
& Pontikoníssia
16 Mon Repos ★

SIGHTSEEING

1 OLD FORTRESS

Start your tour of the city at the Old Venetian Fortress, which offers great views over the city. After that, you'll know your way around! You will be treated to splendid views over the whole town if you wander up the first of the fortress's two hills – you can quench your thirst afterwards at the café. Although resembling an Ancient Greek masterpiece, the temple in front of you was in fact built by the British: the former Anglican St George's Church is modelled on a Doric temple. On leaving the fortress, you will have a good view from the bridge over the artificial moat, the *Contrafossa*, which some Corfiots use as their weekend retreat and keep simple huts in which they store their barbecues and fishing gear. *May–Oct daily 8am–8pm, Nov–April daily 8:30am–3:30pm | admission 6 euros, combined ticket 14 euros, after that, free until 2am – but without access to the summit |* ⏱ *1 hour |* 🔲 *c5–6*

2 CASA PARLANTE 🎏

Seeing is believing! This "talking house" in the old town invites you to visit the former home of a noble Corfiot family from around 1830. Tours are organised by a friendly young group of guides who first introduce you to the family members – all animated figures: the father reads international newspapers, the mother drinks some of the finest English tea and the children practise the piano and violin under the watchful eye of their strict governess. You are invited to a glass of liqueur and sweet pastry while taking in the building's sounds and smells. The tour ends by descending into the cramped living quarters of the servants and kitchen. You will return to the 21st century after about 30 minutes. *Daily 10am–8pm | admission 8 euros | Odós N. Theotóki 16 | casaparlante.gr |* 🔲 *e3*

3 ÀGIOS SPIRÍDONAS CHURCH 🚩

The bones of St Spiridon, a Cypriot martyr from around CE 300, are the most important object in Corfu's most-visited church. A noble Corfiot family purchased his remains from a travelling salesman in 1456 – as was common all over Europe in medieval times. Over the centuries, the relics have not only blessed the common folk; they have saved entire cities,

WHERE TO START?

To reach the central **Esplanade** (🔲 e–f3–5), go up to Plátia G. Theotókou (Sarocco Square) from the long-distance bus terminal. This is also the terminus for buses to the nearby beaches. The Odós G. Theotóki that makes its way as Odós Voulgaréos through the Old Town will lead you to your destination: the open square between the Old Fortress, Old Palace and Ionian Academy. It is best to park your car at the Old Port (the Esplanade car park is often full) and walk through the Old Town or along the sea.

The Old Fortress withstood many sieges; today, it is the symbol of Kérkyra

islands and countries from war and helped to contain the spread of the plague and cholera. St Spyridon also exceeded all expectations when he was held responsible for saving Corfu from the hands of the Turks in 1716. He still attracts many followers and believers today.

Believers of all age groups come throughout the day, light a candle, kiss the sarcophagus and write their wishes or thanks to the saint in a book. Silver oil lamps, donated by believers, hang over the sarcophagus. It is easy to recognise that some of them were donated by seamen and ship owners: they are decorated with silver model boats or with votive plates of ship reliefs. Take a seat in the nave on the right to watch the comings and goings. *Open during the day | Odós Spirídonos | ⊙ 10 mins | ⊞ e2–3*

🔴 SYNAGOGUE

Corfu has always been a multicultural society. In the past, it was a mix of Orthodox Corfiots, Catholic Venetians, and Cretans who had fled their home-land from the Turks, as well as the French and British. Today it is tourists (with more than a few Brits and French still among them). Jews were an inte-gral part of the island's population until the Germans came and deported 2,000 members of the Jewish com-munity. Only one of the four synagogues remains today. This 17th-century temple is a place for quiet reflection and remembrance. It can be visited every day except on the Sabbath, and a Greek steward is on hand to provide brief explanations in English on request. *Daily 11am–4pm | admission free | Odós Velissáriou 4 | ⊙ 15 mins | ⊞ c3*

5 NEW FORTRESS (NÉO FROÚRIO)

All good things come in threes. Even if you have already seen the Old Town of Corfu from the Old Fortress and the Cavalieri Roof Garden, you may still want to climb up the New Fort. The New Fort is not at all new, just not quite as old as the Old Fort. The Venetians built it in the 16th century. You will be rewarded with a stylish café on the top of the fortress walls, rarely visited by other tourists.

The adventurous among you will also be treated to several small bars and night clubs dotted around the entrance to the fort. You can check out the evening's programme when you walk by – you may find that something is on that only the locals know about. *June–Sept daily, April/ May, Oct daily 10am–3pm | admission free | entrance Odós Solomú | ⏱ 1h | ⅲ a–b2–3*

INSIDER TIP
Finger on the pulse

6 FALIRÁKI (ÁGIOS NIKÓLAS GATE) ★

Today, this lovely building with the small St Nicholas Chapel on a peninsula north of the Old Fortress is an ideal place to relax on the waterfront with a drink or have a delicious meal. In the 19th century, this was where the steam and sailing ships anchored at the docks, and was often where emigrants departing for America boarded their cross-Atlantic vessels. The boats that sail past the old debarkation point make for great photos – even the

Cambiéllo in the Old Town is full of charming alleyways and surprising details

enormous cruise ships. But be careful – their wash can create waves big enough to soak the quay and the feet of people sitting at the quay-side restaurants. *Usually 8pm–2am (as long as the bars are open) | free access from Odós Arseníu |* 📖 *f1*

⁊ BYZANTINE MUSEUM ★

More than 100 valuable icons from the 15th to 18th centuries from Corfiot houses of worship have found a dignified new home in the *Panagía Antivuniótissa* Church in the Old Town. Soft Byzantine music can be heard in the background while you make your visit. Of the stories these icons tell, two are especially noteworthy. The fourth icon on the left after the cash desk, a traditional Byzantine icon from around 1490, shows St George on a horse with a young boy holding a tea-pot and cup sitting behind him (no. 186). Pirates had abducted the boy and made him their cupbearer. In her sorrow, his mother turned to St George who brought her son back to her. The icon to the left of the west portal is a work by the famous Cretan painter Michaíl Damáskinos from around 1752 in the so-called Cretan style, showing Saints Sérgios, Bákchos and Justini (no. 141). It is believed that they were responsible for the Christian fleet defeating the Turks on their feast day, 7 October, in 1571. They are shown standing on a decapitated three-headed monster symbolising the Turkish fleet.

The life icons portray the hagiography (or *vita*) of St Nicholas telling a series of miracles he performed (no. 186). In ten different scenes, he rescues people at sea, stops the sword of a hangman who wants to execute an innocent man and offers a bag full of money to a poor father who is forced to put his daughter up for prostitution. *Wed–Mon 8.30am–4pm | admission 4 euros, combined ticket 14 euros | steps lead up from Odós Arseníu |* ⊙ *20–30 mins |* 📖 *d1*

⁸ CAMBIÉLLO

Put away your Marco Polo guide now and enjoy an aimless stroll between the sea promenade, Odós Filéllinon, *Odós Ágios Spirídonos* and the Old Palace, through the old town's most beguiling district. Pass by the local stray cats and dogs, walk under the washing lines stretched from window to window and meet the locals who live here. There is no store or *kafenío* around here to distract you. It is purely a residential area where students have found affordable accommodation on the top floors of dilapidated houses and old people are content with gazing down at the streets below because most of the buildings are without lifts. The district is proof that beauty can emerge from poverty, and leaves you pondering which of the top-floor flats in the century-old five and six-storey buildings you would renovate if you had the money. 📖 *e–f3–5*

⁹ ESPLANADE ★

The Esplanade is a hive of activity. Its broad expanse is the centre of all social life, the site of the *vólta* – the traditional promenade held every evening – and occasional military parades; it is a meeting place for young and old, for locals and holidaymakers.

The Venetians created the Esplanade in the 17th century. Until then, the houses in the town reached all the way to the Old Fortress. The army had them torn down to have the unrestricted option of opening fire in the case of a siege. Later, this green area was used as a parade ground, but today cricket is played on the grass. There is a fountain in the shady park. One of the monuments erected here commemorates the unification of the Ionian islands with free Greece in 1864. It shows seven bronze reliefs with symbols of the seven main islands. Corfu is represented by the ship of the Phaeacians, the legendary people that – according to Homer – lived on Corfu and brought Odysseus back to his homeland of Ithaca by ship.

The west side of the Esplanade is flanked by tall, 19th-century houses that are still lived in today. It is lovely to sit in the little armchairs in one of the cafés under their arcades or *liston* – although these establishments are quite pricey.

A cheaper alternative is to picnic on the other side, to the left of the entrance of the Old Fort. In the *Boschetto* park, a table and chairs

The gables in the Archaeological Museum tell a story of their own

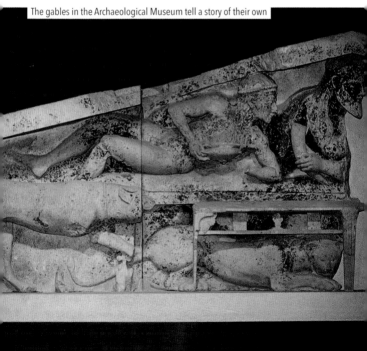

made from palm-tree stumps invite guests to take a picnic surrounded by onlookers. From here it is just a few steps to the *horse-drawn carriages* which line up waiting to take you on a 40-minute tour of the city. Afterwards, you can head up to the rooftop garden bar of the Hotel Cavalieri in the south-west corner of the Esplanade to take in the amazing views of Corfu at night. *e-f3-5*

⑩ MUSEUM OF ASIAN ART/ PALACE OF ST MICHAEL & ST GEORGE ☂

Just beyond the northern end of the Esplanade, the Old Palace was built from 1819 to 1823 by Maltese workers using sandstone they had brought over from Malta. The construction was commissioned by the British to house their Lord High Commissioner, and the three large function rooms facing the Esplanade once hosted parties for the island's British elite and later Greece's Royal Family. The leaders of EU countries also held a conference here in 1994, the renovations for which were financed from EU subsidies.

Asian art, which was collected by well-off Greeks and offered as gifts to their country, is on display in most of the other rooms. Hidden away in one corner of the museum are erotic reliefs portraying acrobatic *Kama Sutra* scenes, taken from the famous temple at the Khajuraho Group of Monuments in India. *Daily 8am–8pm| admission 6 euros, combined ticket 14 euros | Esplanade |* 40–50 mins | *f2*

INSIDER TIP
Not quite PG viewing

⑪ KÍPOS TOU LAOÚ

What do Ground Zero and the public gardens to the south of the Old Palace have in common? Both are memorial sites that invite visitors to touch the plaques and commemorate tragic loss of life. In New York, you can tenderly touch a bronze panel with the names of the 9-11 victims, while on Corfu you can stroke the feather-like wings of the statue that was erected in memory of the 280 Italian officers who were murdered and drowned (by weighing down the corpses with rocks) by the German mountain infantry in 1943. *10 mins | f2*

⑫ ARCHAEOLOGICAL MUSEUM ★

The sight of the horrifying visage of the gorgon Medusa is enough to give anyone a fright. This ancient Greek creature has snakes growing out of her hair and shoulders and hanging round her waist; her eyes appear to be popping out of her head, her tongue is hanging out of her wide mouth. No wonder that the Ancient Greeks believed the sight of her turned the enemy to stone and had this gorgon erected on the gable of their most important temple to ward off thieves and fire.

The museum also exhibits slightly more attractive artefacts: Dionysus, the God of wine and theatre, is engraved into a second smaller gable. There are also several majestic lions. One of the lions dates from the early archaic period around 630 BCE, and is believed to be the first sculpture of a lion in all of Europe. *Nov–March 8.30am–3.30pm Wed–Mon, May–October 8am–8pm Wed–Mon | Odós Wraíla 1 | b6*

🔟 BRITISH CEMETERY

The cemetery, with its colonial tombstones seems like an enchanted park, and it is not only a romantic place but also a great attraction for flower-lovers in spring and autumn with its many wild orchids. *Daily, from sunrise to sunset | Odós Kolokotróni 25 |* ⏱ *20–30 mins |* 🗺 *a–b6*

INSIDER TIP
Wildflower paradise

🔟 PALAIÓPOLIS

The archaeological site of Palaiópolis has been home to numerous key buildings over the centuries. Towards the end of the fifth century, the early Christians on Corfu built a five-aisled church on top of the still distinguishable remains of a small Roman music theatre, or "Odeon". Traces of the theatre can still be seen today. Its floor was originally decorated with magnificent mosaics, and some lovely fragments have been preserved in the exhibition rooms of the Old Fortress. The impressive walls date from a small, Gothic church built during the Venetian period. *Wed–Mon 8.30am–3.30pm | admission free | opposite the entrance to the Castle Park | City bus to Kanóni, Palaiópolis stop |* ⏱ *10–20 mins |* 🗺 *D5*

🔟 AGÍAS EFTHÍMIAS CONVENT

This tranquil Venetian convent is the perfect spot for a spot of meditative respite between Corfu's major attractions. Although situated in the town, *Agía Efímia* is a tiny, idyllic location away from the crowds of tourists and particularly notable for its beautiful flower-filled courtyard. The nuns open up their convent to the public and may even serve you a cup of Greek coffee. *In summer daily 8am–1pm and 5–8pm; at other times 9am–noon and 4–6pm | Anemómilos | on the road from Mon Repos beach to the Palaiópolis Basilica |* ⏱ *10-20 mins |* 🗺 *D5*

🔟 MON REPOS ★

The late Prince Phillip of Greece, who went on to become the husband of Queen Elizabeth II, was once pushed around the enchanting grounds žof Mon Repos in his pram. Born in this small castle on 10 June 1921, there is nothing here to remind you that his family once resided here; the building now houses a varied collection of memorabilia connected to the island's history and flora. Going into the palace is not a must, but you probably won't see another place like it in Greece if you are interested.

Covered in ivy, most of the park's tropical trees are almost 200 years old. For a more unusual experience, take advantage of the little-known fact that you can go swimming in the park. A short walk through the park from the little palace will bring you to a strip of beach and a jetty – a mini green oasis which time appears to have forgotten: 🏖 *Mon Repos beach.*

INSIDER TIP
Don't forge to bring a towel

The remains of two Ancient Greek temples are also dotted around the gardens; the Doric Temple is ideal for a few peaceful moments sitting in the grass or picnicking between the 2,500-year old pillars. *Park daily*

8am–7pm | admission free | museum Wed–Mon 8.30am–4pm | admission 4 euros | entrance at the Palaiópolis stop on the bus route to Kanóni | ⏱ 1–2 hrs | 🗺 D5

🟥 KANÓNI, VLACHÉRNA MONASTERY & PONTIKONÍSSIA

Kanóni's stunning terrace allows you to make an unusual addition to your holiday album by taking photos of planes landing and taking off from the airport. The unparalleled views of the runway are not the only spectacular sight from this lookout. Turn 90 degrees to see Corfu's favourite postcard image: the small islands of *Vlachérna* and *Pontikoníssi* off the coast which – if you'd been able to lean out the window – you probably could almost have touched during your descent by plane. You can walk over to Vlachérna via a small causeway. This land bridge is almost entirely taken up by a now empty monastery, built at the start of the 18th century. Boats also depart from the causeway to the "Mouse Island" (*Pontikoníssi*), where Austria's Empress "Sisi" liked to sit. The small church was built in the 12th century. *Monastery and church are open to the public during the day | city bus line 2 | ⏱ 1.5–2 hrs | 🗺 D 5–6*

🟥 VÍDOS

Interested in a small boat ride? Then take a trip out to the lush, green outcrop of Vídos. There are two ways of reaching the island: an affordable ferry service from the Old Port makes the crossing in just a few minutes, or the more expensive *Calypso Star*. You can

Just a few steps further to reach the tip of the monastery island of Vlachérna

The Esplanade is atmospheric in the evening

walk across the island in 40 minutes, following the well-signposted paths, to reach a couple of tiny pebble beaches and also discover that the island is an important pilgrim site for Serbs. Ten thousand Serbian soldiers were quarantined on the island by the enemy troops in World War I, and many died of hunger and epidemics. Their descendants erected a memorial on Vídos to commemorate their loved ones. *Daily 10am–midnight | return trip 2.20 euros | Calypso Star every hour 10am–6pm | departure from the same jetty at the Old Port | 15 euros | 🕮 D5*

EATING & DRINKING

AEGLI

Have you ever been invited to dine with a diplomat? The owner of this exclusive restaurant is no less than the Honorary Consul of Germany, who combines his official title with his gastronomic activities. Although none of the guests wear ties or evening dresses, this fine-dining establishment boasts linen napkins, white tablecloths and highly professional service. Reservations are required. *Daily | Odós I. Kapodístrias 13 | Esplanade | tel. 26 61 03 19 49 | €€€ | 🕮 e2*

BELLISSIMO

Father and son, Kóstas and Stávros, take care of front of house, while Ánna and Dóra are in charge of the kitchen. There are five to six different home-made specialities every day along with *gyros* and grilled meat. *Spanakópitta*, home-made puff pastry filled with chard, mint, leek, a bit of cheese and

INSIDER TIP
Poetry in pastry

touch of fennel, is pure poetry. Meals are served on a pretty, newly laid-out, square. *Mon–Sat, in August also Sun evening | Odós D. Bitzárou Kyriaki | entrance between 67 and 69 Odós N. Theotóki | €€ | ▥ d3*

EKTÓS SKÉDIO
In this appropriately named "no plan" restaurant, the waiter brings you a hand-written menu along with an order card where you can enter what you'd like to eat, preferably in Greek but English will do. Your *mezedákia* then arrives in batches of small portions which are placed in the middle of the table for everyone to help themselves. If you run out of food, you can simply ask the waiter for seconds. The Corfiots love to choose what and how they want to eat – free tables are scarce after 10pm. *Mon–Sat only in the evening | Odós Prossaléndiou 43 | behind the Court building | €€ | ▥ c2*

GYROS SOUVLKÁKI GRILL HOUSE 🐖
There aren't many tables at this popular alleyway spot so getting one can be quite a challenge. It's worth it though for delicious *gyros* served either in pitta breads or as part of platters with some salad and tzatzíki – all at a seriously fair price. *Mon–Sat 6pm-midnight | Odós Prossaléndou | € | ▥ c2*

KÁTHE PRÁMA STON KAIRÓ TOU
This restaurant is just as unusual as its name, which translates as "Everything in good time". The owner, Spíros, is an artistic chef who offers individual interpretations of traditional Greek dishes. His mussels in muscatel are a dream, as are the lamb meatballs served on a bed of aubergine puree. *Daily | Odós Mitropóleos 22 | €€ | ▥ d2*

O KRITIKÓS
Corfu's premier spot for cakes and confectionery has plenty of tables inside, which means you can spend a while comfortably thinking about just how good the walnut cake is! *Platía Saróccо| € | ▥ b6*

OLD FORTRESS CAFÉ
The modern café in the Old Fortress is an atmospheric location to drink excellent Greek wines, cocktails or *tsípouro* (grappa) accompanied by an omelette, salad or platter of mixed starters, *pikilies*. There are concerts on some evenings. *Daily | in the Old Fortress (see p. 42) | admission only with a valid ticket when the Old Fortress is open; after that, free | €€€ | ▥ c6*

PÉRGOLA
Sákis, the owner of this unpretentious taverna, serves the best Greek food, slightly sparkling wine from the village of Zitsa on the mainland and excellent grappa. Stuffed aubergines with a cheese topping and his salad of wild greens *tsigarélli* are heavenly. *Daily | Odós Agías Sofias 10 | €€ | ▥ c3*

ROÚVAS 🐖
There is no outdoor seating in this typical market taverna, but here you can choose your meal directly from the pots of – mostly – stewed dishes. The

salads are fresh and crisp, and the vegetables and meat come from the market. Many stallholders eat here – they know what quality is! *Mon–Sat 9am–5pm | Odós Dessíla 13 | € | ▢ c4*

ROSY'S BAKERY
The brainchild of Rosy Soussis, this little bakery specialises in gluten-free and vegetarian snacks. It has only been going for a few years, but the number of delicious things on offer is extraordinary and grows every year! *Daily 10am–11.30pm | Odós Palaiologou 94 | € | ▢ c4*

TABERNITA MEXICANA
Tables and chairs are spread out over several small terraces and lawn areas of this establishment's garden, either in the sun or under shady trees. The Greek-Canadian couple who own the tavern specialise in excellent steaks and Mexican cuisine, but also have pizza and Greek dishes on their menu. Guests are welcome to drink just a coffee, cocktails or a selection of tequilas. *Daily | Odós Solomoú 31 | near the entrance to the New Fort | €€ | ▢ b3*

SHOPPING

The main shopping streets for the locals are *Odós Vularéos* in the Old Town and its continuation, 👆*Odós G. Theotóki*, in the new section with its beautiful arcades. Modern shops, especially those selling electrical items and multimedia, can be found on the wide *Odós Aléxandras* that runs from *Platía G. Theotóki* (Sarocco Square) to the sea. Arts and crafts and souvenirs are mainly offered on *Odós N. Theotóki, Odós Filarmonikís* and *Odós Filéllinon* in the Old Town. There are also many small shops on *Odós Ag. Sofías* in the old Jewish quarter.

BLANC DU NIL (▢ C2)
Do you like wearing white? Then you've found your vegan clothing paradise in this boutique: fashionable clothes for both him and her, exclusively in white and made from the finest Egyptian cotton. You don't have to start planning your wedding though; "white nights" are popular theme nights in many Corfu clubs. *Odós Agíon Pándon 20 | Old Port | ▢ c2*

BY TOM ▶
Are you fed up with all the plastic in your kitchen? If so, Thomás Koumarákos is your man. Thomás only uses traditional techniques, and has been putting his heart and soul into his work since he started in 1969. He makes everything from chopping boards, salad servers and bowls to egg cups. Visitors will enjoy the mesmerising smell of wood from his workshop, and his collection of tools is no less impressive. He revels in making bespoke pieces for his customers within a few hours

INSIDER TIP
Custom-made souvenirs

and at a reasonable price. *Parodós N. Theotóki 3i | entrance between the houses at 81 and 83 | ▢ c2*

LALAÓUNIS
Greece's most renowned jeweller, Ilias Lalaóunis, not only has branches in

New York and on the Virgin Islands, but also in Corfu's Old Town selling beautiful gold pieces. *Odós Kapodistríu 35 | on the northwest corner of the arcades on the Esplanade |* ⌖ *e3*

PATOUNIS

If you buy Patounis's beautifully wrapped soap once, the chances are you will at some point come back for more. A family business going back five generations, the Patounises produce soap made from olive oil in five different varieties.

> **INSIDER TIP**
> **Visit a soapmaker**

There is a tour through the small factory every day (except Sundays) at 12. *Mon–Sun 9.30am–2pm, Tue, Thu, Fri also 6–8.30pm | Odós Theotóki 9 |near Platía Sarócco*

VASSILÁKIS 🚩

Are you looking for a souvenir that you can find only on Corfu? Then look no further than the kumquat (or *koum kouat*), a citrus fruit grown exclusively on the island. This edible fruit, closely resembling the orange, is added to liqueur, ouzo and brandy, or made into sweets and jams. Its scent is even used for perfumes. Nikos Vassilákis and his staff will let you try all the items on sale. *Daily 8am–midnight | Odós Spirídonos 61|* ⌖ *e2*

VELVET

Greek women's fashion designers are a rarity on Corfu, but a few are on display here, in particular the labels Veloudákis and Zinás. *Odós N. Theotóki 42 |* ⌖ *d3*

Liqueurs in pretty bottles are available at Vassilákis

WEEKLY MARKET

A real market with regional products! You won't find any souvenirs here, but things the locals need every day: fresh fish, pulses, nuts, fruit and vegetables, herbs and flowers. There are small cafés between the stands, and the proprietors even take coffee to the stallholders; lottery ticket sellers promise big prizes... *Mon–Sat 6am–2pm | in the moat beneath Odós Sp. Vlaikoj | ▥ b4*

SPORT & ACTIVITIES

Sport fans will find their fun elsewhere on Corfu, but there are plenty of outdoor activities to keep kids occupied in Corfu town. Many of these can be found in the evening on the southern side of the Esplanade.

If your children dream of being the next Lewis Hamilton, they can try their hands at driving with the 🚗 electric cars here. So long as they can grip a steering wheel and reach the peddles, they can buckle in and put their foot down. Rides cost about 3 euros.

🚗 A few metres from the cars is the "station" for the town's tourist trains (*8 euros, children 5–12 5 euros*). The ride lasts around 35 minutes and the trains set off every hour between 10am and 9pm.

BEACHES

A dip in the sea can easily be combined with a sundowner in a beach bar in the centre of town. However, the swimming is more attractive at the resort of ⋆ *Faliráki*, where the sun

loungers are free for guests at the *Imabári (see p. 55)* beach bar. A more traditional spot is the ⋆ *Mon Repos Lido* (▥ D5) at the southern end of the promenade. Both lidos offer fresh water showers and cubicles.

Corfiots are not especially picky about where they swim but find spots all along the coast from the Old Fortress to the small beacon on the pier at *Garitsa*. The beach opposite Mouse Island on the spit at *Kanóni* is also worth a trip.

WELLNESS

After a day traipsing around town, your feet will likely be in need of some TLC. Luckily, Corfu Town is well set-up in this regard, with a large number of fish spas dotted in its centre. These floating masseurs await your arrival... hungrily. *Fish Spa* (▥ d3) (*Odós N. Theotoki 47 | daily 10am–10pm | Prices from 10 euros*)

NIGHTLIFE

To the relief of locals, the island's party mile is located away from residential areas, on the coastal road between the New Port and the city bypass. There is no regular bus service in the evenings so most partygoers take a taxi home. Except for a few stalwarts, the pubs and clubs along this mile change hands (and names) regularly. Nonetheless, most offer free admission and the same style of Greek music; not *syrtáki* though, but metal, rock and the like. Those who prefer to stay in the Old Town should head up to the New Fort; there is a good nightlife scene around the fort's entrance.

CAVALIERI ROOF GARDEN ★

A conservative venue offering sensational views – the rooftop bar at the Hotel Cavalieri is a good location early evening, despite its expensive prices. *Daily from 6pm | no admittance in shorts | Odós Kapodistríu 4 | ⊞ e5*

54 DREAMY NIGHTS

The hippest club (when we last checked...) on Corfu plays mainly deep house, hip-hop and Greek mainstream. The club's owners are particularly proud of their high-tech light shows and live music concerts. It usually attracts some of the town's VIPs, who arrive in their sports cars rather than take a taxi home. *Leofóros Ethn. Antistáseos 54 | 54dreamynights. com | ⊞ D5*

GRAAL

The alternative night spot playing jazz, jam and Latin swing and hosting the occasional live concert. The evening kicks off relatively early: from 10pm onwards crowds gather inside and outside directly under the walls of the New Fort. *Odós Solomoú 34 facebook. com/graal.eraldicon | ⊞ b3*

IMABÁRI ★

Chillax is the portmanteau to describe this seaside lounge bar named, for no explicable reason, after a Japanese town. The sun loungers become "moon loungers" in the evening, and if temperatures refuse to drop, you can cool down by dipping your feet into

You can sunbathe on the pier at Faliráki or on a free sunbed at the beach

Achíllion is Corfu's most famous sight and was a place of refuge for Imperial rulers

the sea. The designer cocktails are the best in town and the chef offers a small yet fine menu with creative Corfiot touches. *Daily from 9am | Faliráki Beach | ▥ f1*

POLYTÉCHNO

The hotspot for alternative partygoers. The club specialises in experimental music and also hosts stand-up comedy nights, cartoon festivals and "*koktéli naits*" when rum takes centre stage. Get there by 9.30pm to gain entry. The programme of events is posted on

INSIDER TIP
Hipster scene

Facebook and on the board outside the club next to the entrance. *Odós Solomoú/Oddós Schoulemvoúrgou (New Fort) | tel. 26 61 02 77 94 | facebook.com/polytechnocorfu | ▥ b3*

YARD CLUB

This club specialises in theme nights. The best parties from Athens are repeated here on Wednesdays while the weekend brings "eKlectric Friday" and "Get so hot" on Saturdays with R'n'B. The Yard Club has been a stalwart on Corfu's clubbing scene for years. *Leofóros Ethn. Antistáseos 52 | facebook.com/Yard-Club | ▥ D5*

AROUND CORFU TOWN

ACHÍLLION ★

Emperors can be eccentric folk. The last Kaiser of Germany was certainly a bit of a funny fish. Wilhelm II liked to sit on a stool shaped like a cavalry saddle – an oddity exhibited here as well as in the Netherlands where he was sent to exile. You are left wondering whether he signed the declaration to World War I while swaying to and fro on this rocking horse saddle. The Kaiser hero-worshipped the figure of "victorious Achilles" and had a monument built in his memory with his helmet, shield and lance. The statue stands in the splendid gardens, which the Kaiser bought, along with the castle, in 1907. Until the onset of World War I, he spent Easter here with his family and red Mercedes car. The building of the castle was, in fact, commissioned by the Empress Elisabeth of Austria (1837–98), who regularly visited her beloved Corfu from 1891 until her assassination in Geneva. She also loved this Ancient Greek hero but, in keeping with her melancholic nature, chose to portray the "dying Achilles" in her garden statue. *May–Oct daily 8.30am–7pm; at other times Tue–Sun 8.45am–3.30pm | admission 7 euros*

You can taste the wines and liqueurs made by the *Vassilákis* distillery opposite *Achíllion. There are four to six buses daily to Achíllion – more in the high season – from San Rocco Square (line 10); tickets, also for the return trip, must be purchased in advance at the* bus station or a kiosk; tickets are not available on the bus | 8km / 5 miles) from Kérkyra | ⏱ 1–1.5 hrs | �🗺 D6

BETTER PLACES TO STAY IN CORFU TOWN

BELLA VENEZIA

Pretty posh. Ever stayed in a neo-Classicist building that was once a bank and then a girls' boarding school. If not, the atmospheric *Bella Venezia* is for you. Each room is different, and most have small balconies. Breakfast is served in the garden pavilion; the small bar opposite the lobby is the place to have an apéritif or nightcap in a relaxed environment. *32 rooms | Odós Zambelíu 4 | tel. 26 61 04 65 00 | bellaveneziahotel. com | €€€ | �🗺 d5*

ELEVATOR ADVENTURE

Are you always on the lookout for an adventure? Then check into the *Konstantinoúpolis*, the oldest hotel in town, complete with its antiquated lift. In spite of its age, the lift has always been reliable over the years, transporting a maximum of two people without luggage (or one person with) to the rooms above. Here you will be woken up by the sound of the Greek national anthem coming from the nearby marine station when the Greek flag is hoisted. *34 rooms | Odós K. Zavitsianoú 11 | tel. 26 61 04 87 16 | booking via booking.com | €€ | �🗺 c1*

THE NORTH

BEACHES, TEMPLES AND MUCH, MUCH MORE

Although the whole of Corfu is beautiful, many believe the island's north to be its jewel. If you hire a car for just one or two days, make sure you explore this region. The roads will take you on a rollercoaster ride, as the landscape rolls through the hills – take your foot off the gas and take in the views! The hiking around here is superb and there is a lot to explore at sea too.

The region is defined by the massif formed by the island's highest peak, Pantokrátoras (906m / 3000ft), and the steep bays along the

Cape Drástis

coast. Pretty little coves line the west coast below the coastal road, which runs round the entire island. A 6-km / 4-mile long beach stretches along the north coast from Róda to beyond Acharávi. And in the west, you can bathe on narrow strips of sand clinging to steep, rugged cliffs or in the crescent-shaped bay of Ágios Geórgios. Venture through the ancient olive groves to discover old villages full of historic buildings that take you back in time. Visiting some of the many ancient landmarks in the region will round off your exploration of the north.

THE NORTH

Cape Drástis ★
Canal d'Amour

8 Astrakéri

7 Sidári

6 Peroulades

Róda
p. 66

Αυλιώτες
Avliotes

Γουσάδες
Gousades

Καβαλλούρι
Kaballouri

Σφα
Sfake

Λιβάδι
Livadi

Αγραφοί
Agrafi

Ágios Stéfanos
p. 75

Μαγουλάδες
Magoulades

Βελονάδες
Velonades

Άγιοι Δούλοι
Agii Douli

10 Nímfe

Arillas
p. 75

Αρμενάδες
Armenades

Μεσαριά
Mesaria

Άγιοι Δούλοι
Agii Douli

Κλη
Klim

Βαλανείο
Valanio

Δάφνη
Dafni

Afiónas ★
p. 75

Αγρός
Agros

Χωρεπίσκοποι
Chorepiskopi

Timióni Beach

Ágios Geórgios
p. 75

Αρκαδάδες
Arkadades

37km, 60 mins

Σκριπερό
Skripero

Βίστωνας
Vistonas

Makrádes **15**

Δουκάδες
Doukades

GREECI

Lákones **14**

Angelókastro ★ **16**

Paleokastrítsa
p. 77

Λιαπάδες
Liapades

Ionio

Κανακάδες
Kanakades

25km, 40 mins

Pelagos

Γιαννάδες
Giannades

Corfu Tov

2 km
1.24 mi

Ερμόνες
Ermones

Almirós Beach   Agía Ekateríni   Ágios Spirídonas Beach

13

Acharávi
p. 66

17km, 25 mins

10km, 40 mins

Άγιος Ηλίας
Ágios Elias

Λούτσες
Loutses

Batería Beach

Kassiópi ★
p. 62

Άγιος Παντελεήμονας
Ágios Pantaleimonas

12 Paleó Períthia ★

Ágios Stéfanos Siniés **1**

Επίσκεψη
Episkepsi

11 Pantokrátor ★

Κερασιά
Kerasia

9 Strinílas

3 Koulоúra
4 Kalámi

2 Agní

Σγουράδες
Sgourades

Σπαρτύλας
Spartílas

5 Kamináki Beach

υγός
ygos

Άγιος Μάρκος
Ágios Markos

Μπαρμπάτι
Barbati

Κάτω Άγιος Μάρκος
Kato Agios Markos

37km, 55 mins

Ύψος
Ipsos

**Kérkyra
(Korfu)**

Δασσία
Dassia

Corfu Town

MARCO POLO HIGHLIGHTS

★ **KASSIÓPI**
The island's most picturesque coastal
resort ➤ p. 62

★ **CAPE DRÁSTIS**
First the fairy-tale panorama and then a
refreshing dip ➤ p. 71

★ **PANTOKRÁTOR**
Drive up to the island's highest peak
➤ p. 72

★ **PALEÓ PERÍTHIA**
A village left as it was in Venetian days
and a rustic taverna far away from any
traffic noise ➤ p. 73

★ **AFIÓNAS**
Picture-perfect village with two beaches
and fantastic tavernas ➤ p. 75

★ **ANGELÓKASTRO**
Romantic castle ruins high above a wild
coastal scene ➤ p. 81

Αgios Ioannis   Alepou

KASSIÓPI

(⎕ D2) ★ **Kassiópi is different. Unlike your run-of-the-mill beach resorts, this coastal village has a permanent population of 1,100 inhabitants, and such is the place's buzz that you almost get the feeling that they could survive pretty well without tourism.**

From the village there is no beach or large hotel in sight. Instead, you are treated to a picturesque harbour and narrow lanes bursting with tavernas and bars, as well as an authentic *kafenio*. There is even a tiny *platía* with everything you could ever need, from a bus stop to a post office. On closer look, you'll discover the remains of the Venetian fortress walls towering up between the trees above the harbour buildings – and the rectory on the roof of the village church. Now you're probably curious. Take your time to explore this little gem.

SIGHTSEEING

CASTLE (KASTRO)

Over the past few years, the EU has invested millions in the castle that the Venetians built in 1386 on top of the remains of an old fortress. This investment and the marketing that has accompanied it has transformed the

A great place for eating and relaxing: the seafront restaurants at Kassiópi

castle into an important part of any tourist's itinerary. But what has the money paid for? Well, at night, the interior – completely overgrown by scrub and mainly a glorified pen for local sheep and chickens – is lit up, and there is a brand-new sprinkler system to ensure everyone's safety on their short visits. To be fair, the gatehouse has also been restored and improvements made to the outer walls with their 13 towers. Nonetheless, whether this is the right kind of financial aid Greece needs remains debatable. *Free access | the path to the castle begins on the main road to the harbour opposite Panagía Kassiópitra Church*

PANAGÍA KASSIÓPITRA CHURCH

Although today's priests no longer need to stagger up to the roof of their church at the end of a hard day's work, their predecessors' rectory is very much a part of the building. Although the rectory is closed to the public, the church is open every day. It was built in 1590 on the site of an ancient Roman temple frequented by the likes of the mad Emperor Nero and Cicero. Rumour even has it that Cleopatra crossed its threshold. That's because in ancient Greek and medieval times, Kassiópi was a popular stop-off for ships sailing between Greece and Italy. After a stormy crossing from the boot of Italy, travellers could recuperate here from a bout of seasickness or wait until the waters were calmer to attempt the return journey. *Generally open 9am–noon | Access from the main road to the harbour and the* *terrace of the The Old School tavern at the harbour*

JÁNIS

The white-blossoming yucca palms in late summer are reason enough to visit one of the resort's largest tavernas. Although primarily catering for British guests, the dishes try to give tourists a taste of authentic Greek food by offering Corfiot-style *mezedákia* with lots of small portions of fresh food brought to the table.

> **INSIDER TIP**
> Eat like a Corfiot

These small dishes allow you to branch out from the more standard tourist fare. *Daily | where the one-way road from the harbour meets the circular island road | €€€*

TAVERNÁKI

Searching for the perfect location for a romantic dinner for two? Then look no further than this delightful taverna. Designed in natural stone and wood, the building is decorated with flowers and candlelight to set the romantic mood. Besides the usual tourist menu, the restaurant also serves more creative dishes, such as dried-cod fish cakes. It is advisable to book a table due to the restaurant's popularity. *Daily | eastern side of the harbour basin | tel. 26 63 08 15 29 | €€*

At *Avláki Beach*, the *Corfu Sailing Centre (tel. 69 34 30 50 47 | corfusailingcentre.com)* specialises in

THE FISH CULT

For Corfiots, the sea is more than just scenery – it's also their pantry. At home, they usually eat small, inexpensive fish, but when they go out, only the best is good enough. And they always order more than they can eat.

Fish are objects of devotion here; they have significance as the symbol of Christ and as a healthy food. These are just two of the reasons why fish farming is one of the most important economic pillars on the Ionian Islands. There are more than 500 Greek fish farms which deliver to restaurants and markets in Germany and Italy. Fish that are not to be found in local waters are imported from Thailand, Indonesia and South America. This often means that the prawns the Greeks love so much are no fresher than in many countries in northern Europe.

If you want to try regional fish, you should limit yourself to small *gópes*, *gávri* and *marídes*. These are often caught by small trawlers sailing from Corfiot harbours.

windsurfing and sailing courses, but also has equipment, SUP boards and kayaks for hire. Corfu's first motor boat rental agency fills the harbour of Kassiópi with its motor boats. Those without a boat licence have to settle for a 30hp boat to ride the waves. Boats are available from *Filíppos Rent-a-boat (tel. 26 63 08 12 27 | filippos-boats.com)*, and kayaks and paddle boats can also be hired on Batería Beach. Scuba-diving courses are organised by *Corfu Divers (on the main road | tel. 26 63 02 92 26 | corfu-divers.com)*

BEACHES

Five minutes on foot from the north end of the harbour, at the tip of the castle peninsula, is the 80m / 260ft *Batería Beach*. Deckchairs and umbrellas are available to hire on the coarse sandy beach as well as under the olive trees around the bay. From the south end of the harbour, a small path leads you to a few rocky outcrops where you can also sunbathe. The coarse sandy *Main Beach* skirts Kassiópi's north-western bay near the Jánis taverna. The most beautiful beach is the *Avláki Beach* (a pebbly beach 500m / 1640ft long) to the south, which takes 30 minutes to reach on foot from Kassiópi.

WELLNESS

Kiki Lekka (tel. 69 70 47 10 01) | soultouch.gr) is a native of the island and offers both medical and spa massages in guests' hotel rooms or apartments.

NIGHTLIFE

There are no discos or clubs in Kassiópi. Evenings are spent at the seafront bars, on the *platía* or at *Kóstas Bar* on the road between the harbour and village square where Greek dancing is held every evening from 10pm.

AROUND KASSIÓPI

1 ÁGIOS STÉFANOS SINIÉS
6km (3.7 miles) / about 15 mins by car from Kassiópi

Ágios Stéfanos Siniés (pop. 230) is the closest Corfiot village to Albania which may or may not be reason enough to drive down to this tiny village. If not, maybe one of the island's best fish restaurants can entice you? Some of the tables and chairs of the *Eucalyptus (daily | €€€)* are positioned directly on the beach. You choose your fish from the glass counter and the waiters are experts in the art of removing the bones before serving it. The neighbouring tables are normally occupied by sailors who have anchored their yachts in the secluded bay. *E3*

2 AGNÍ
11km (6.8 miles) / about 20 mins by car from Kassiópi

Agní is a small, peaceful bay with a 150-m / 492-ft-long, white shingle-and-stone beach, a few private rooms and three tavernas. Wooden jetties where yachts moor jut out into the water. The three inns all serve good fresh fish. There are many dishes for vegetarians on the menu of the *Agní tavern (daily | €)* – *marída jemistá* (sardines filled with cheese, garlic and parsley) are quite innovative. Scampi pilaf, *piláfi me gárides*, is the hit in

Batería Beach in Kassiopi may be narrow, but it boasts a beautiful location

Toula's Taverna (daily | €). **Use the car park on the outskirts of the village; it is often impossible to do a u-turn at the seafront!**

INSIDER TIP
Avoid embarrassing u-turns

𝄢 D3

🖪 KOULOÚRA

10km (6.2 miles) / about 20 mins by car from Kassiópi

The semi-oval harbour basin in front of the fortified 16th-century stately home in Kouloúra is one of Corfu's standard postcard images. It is worth taking a photo but a waste of time driving down to the harbour where there are hardly any parking spaces. The house has belonged to an Italian family since 1986 and is off-limits to holidaymakers. *𝄢 E3*

🖪 KALÁMI

11km (6.8 miles) / about 20 mins by car from Kassiópi

The tiny hamlet of Kalámi on the coast has almost been smothered by a large holiday club complex – and with it much of the village's beauty has been lost. However, for fans of the Durrell family, it is worth a pilgrimage. In the 1930s – when the village looked quite different – Kalámi is where they lived. Their home then, the *White House (tel. 26 63 09 10 40 | white-house-corfu. gr | €)*, can be rented as a holiday house; the Durrell family's dining table is still there! There is now a good taverna on the ground floor *(daily | €)*. The 250-m / 820-ft-long pebbly beach is relatively small for so many summer holidaymakers. However, there is a track from here to *Gialiskári Beach* in the north where there are a lot less people on the pebbly beach and rocks. This beach also provides access to an interesting underwater world for snorkelers. *𝄢 E3*

🖪 KAMINÁKI BEACH

17km (10 miles) / about 30 mins by car from Kassiópi

A hidden gem, this photogenic shingle beach, measuring just 100m / 328ft by 15m / 49ft, lies in front of a tiny coastal settlement with two tavernas *(€)* and a water-sports business *(kaminakiboats.com)* that also rents out motorboats without a skipper. There are around 60 loungers under 30 sunshades on the beach, but there is always enough space for your towel if you prefer. *𝄢 D3*

ACHARÁVI & RÓDA

(𝄢 C2) **Are you looking for the ultimate beach holiday? Then the beach resorts of Acharávi (pop. 650) and Róda (pop. 370), which virtually merge together along the north coast, are a perfect choice of destination.**

At 6km / 3.7 miles long and up to 30m / 100ft wide, this stretch of sand is virtually deserted in parts while crowded with parasols and sun loungers in others. Beach bars congregate around the centres and there is always a taverna in close vicinity. The resorts are packed with large all-inclusive

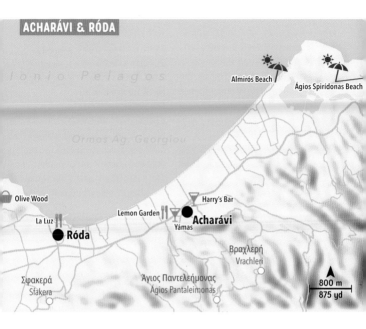

ACHARÁVI & RÓDA

Almirós Beach
Ágios Spiridonas Beach

Ionio Pelagos

Ormos Ag. Georgiou

Olive Wood
Harry's Bar
Lemon Garden
La Luz
Acharávi
Yámas
Róda
Βραχλερή
Vrachleri
Σφακερά
Sfakera
Άγιος Παντελεήμονας
Ágios Pantaleimonás

800 m
875 yd

hotels, as well as affordable holiday flats and properties which attract a colourful mix of holidaymakers – although Brits and Germans dominate. Over the years Corfiots have relocated to the inland villages and only visit the coast in summer. Olive groves stretch up behind the villages to the 900-m / 3,000-ft high Mount Pantokrátoras. Off the coast stand the Diapontia Islands and the rocky Albanian mainland on the other side. You don't necessarily need to hire a car; a bike is a fun way to explore the region or buses run several times a day between both resorts and the island's capital as well as to the neighbouring villages of Kassiópi and Sidári. There is definitely enough to see and do on your beach holiday.

What differentiates the two resorts?

Acharávi is the larger of the two, and its main shopping mile is located directly on the island's busy thoroughfare. Branching off from this main road are dozens of small lanes leading down to the beach, none of which have street names but are numbered. There is no promenade as such and you need to walk along the sand to get from one beach bar to the next.

In contrast, Róda has a tiny centre along the seafront lined with restaurants and bars.

SIGHTSEEING

There are no sights as such in the region as history has barely left its mark here. The resorts are not really idyllic, and only come to life in summer with the crowds of holidaymakers,

EATING & DRINKING

LEMON GARDEN

Even paradise has its flaws. Although lemons appear to be growing in every corner of the Lemon Garden restaurant, the fruits are too sour to eat. The trees however offer welcome shade in the hot summer heat. The restaurant's owner, Soúla, never stops working from early morning to late into the night. A Greek folklore show is held twice a week where guests are taught traditional Greek dances, and there is a Latin American night once a week. Meat and fish are grilled outside in the garden under a traditional Corfiot wooden roof. Make sure you have time for an aperitif; the bar staff mix the best cocktails around.

The family makes many of the products themselves: the strudel dough, limoncello and lemon marmalade. To resist the temptation of picking the lemons in this garden of paradise, take one for free from the baskets full of fruit (picked elsewhere!) at the exit. *Acharávi | on the main road 50m / 164ft to the west of the roundabout | €€*

LA LUZ

One of the most exciting new spots in the north of the island, La Luz offers a modern approach to Greek cooking, with big portions and interesting sides. They also have a range of authentically Greek cocktails. To sample some of the local kumquat liqueur, try the "Marilyn Passion", or the "Eternal Sunshine", which contains Mastiha from Chios. The setting isn't bad either – you can either sit on the beach itself, or on the terrace of the village's oldest building.

INSIDER TIP
Innovative cocktails

PÁNGALOS

Tables on the terrace of the more than 180-year-old, repurposed warehouse are right on the shore. No other restaurant in Róda has a better location, but the food is – like everywhere else in Róda – average at best. *Daily from 11am | Róda | on the coastal road in the village centre | €€*

PUMPHOUSE

A real restaurant with real tablecloths, the glow of tea lights, fresh flowers on the tables and easy-listening music in the background. Many dishes are served with tasty roast potatoes and the well-spiced *tas kebab*, a kind of stew with three types of meat, is outstanding. Large portions. *Daily from noon | Acharávi | at the roundabout | €€€*

SHOPPING

OLIVE WOOD

'Grown to be a bike' was what the Corfu-born Polychrónis first thought on seeing a piece of olive wood, so he transformed it into a Harley Davidson. The life-size motorbike now hangs

There's plenty of space on the beach at Acharávi – even in high season

from the ceiling of his workshop, along with a parrot who likes chatting to customers. As does Paulien, the wood carver's Dutch wife, who speaks several languages and explains how Polychrónis painstakingly makes household and decorative objects from olive wood. *On the road from the Dímitra supermarket to the beach, beach access no. 6 | Acharávi*

SPORT & ACTIVITIES

In Róda, you can join guided horse-riding tours. They last two hours and set off at 9am, 11am, 5pm or 7pm. The meeting point is a paddock between the road that goes around the island and the seafront. *S-Bikes* (see p.33) also offer guided mountain-bike tours almost every day, and you can hire bikes for the day here too. There are several companies offering water sports on the quayside at Róda or in front of the major hotels in Acharávi.

BEACHES

The sandy beach is more than 6km / 3.7 miles long, with only a few pebbly patches. It begins in Róda, makes its way past Acharávi and continues as ✶ *Almirós Beach* to the small island of *Agia Ekaterini* which can be reached over a footbridge. A 30-minute walk along a track will take you across the island to ✶ *Ágios Spirídonas* and, after another 15 minutes, you will reach the road around the island. You can then catch the bus back to Acharávi or Róda.

WELLNESS

There are lots of masseuses in Acharávi and Róda who go around the beaches offering their services. If you are looking for something a bit more special, the island's most beautiful spa is in *St George's Country Club Hotel (country-club.cc)* in Acharávi.

Non-residents need to call in advance to book treatments.

NIGHTLIFE

HARRY'S BAR

"What's a bar without music?" says Harry. He also knows that a sports bar without the constant drone of football commentators in the background is not a sports bar. This explains the mixture of German and British voices, goal celebrations and the greatest hits from the Beatles and Rolling Stones coming from the bar's terrace filled with flowers and wide screens. Guests flock to this pub to enjoy the friendly service of Harry's daughter and Harry himself, who is known for his authenticity and charm, as well as for serving free shots to his guests. *Acharávi | at the eastern end of the old village road | harrysbar-apartments.com*

YÁMAS

This is the place to go if you're looking for a nightcap in Acharávi and Róda. But there is no guarantee that this pub will be open. *Acharávi, at the roundabout*

AROUND AÇHARÁVI & RÓDA

◳ PEROULÁDES

16km (10 miles) / a good hour on bike from Acharávi

Have no fear, the skywalk at Perouládes (pop. 780) is strong enough to bear many a tourist. You will be treated to thrilling views of the narrow sandy beach stretching below

According to local lore, whoever swims through the Canal d'Amour will be lucky in love

the cliffs. Steps lead down to the beach from the car park in front of the open-air bar *Panórama (daily | €€–€€€)* Charging relatively expensive prices, the bar offers seating on its spacious lawn or at tables directly on the cliff's edge. The restaurant, *7th Heaven (daily | €€€)*, serves, if not heavenly, then good food next door.

Make sure to visit ★ *Cape Drástis* beforehand! Of all Corfu's beautiful coastal landscapes, this one at the far north-west tip of the island is the nicest. The white sandstone cliffs on the island's north-western cape are almost 100m / 300ft high. From the cliffs, a series of stunning jagged sandstone rock formations descend to a small bay, where a little rocky island juts out of the water like a shark's fin. The path begins at the clearly recognisable primary school along the village road. There is initially a slight incline, after

which it runs down to the sea and then, all of a sudden, you have the picture-book panorama of the bay in front of you. You can continue following the track by car, jeep, bike or on foot until it ends in a tiny bay surrounded by rocks. If the sea is calm, you can jump into the water here and enjoy a swim in the crystal-clear sea with a view of the steep, light-coloured cliffs that tower up right out of the water. *A2*

INSIDER TIP
For strong swimmers

☷ SIDÁRI
8km (5 miles) / 10 mins by bus from Acharávi

Sidári (pop. 400) is like a fairground; there is a string of bars, travel agencies and souvenir shops along the main street – nothing is left of its former charm. The lingua franca is only Greek in winter; in summer, everyone speaks English. The pools are flooded with rock music and there is hardly a bar that doesn't have a large screen for sporting events. If it wasn't for the heat, you could be forgiven for thinking you were back in the UK.

But there is a different, more picturesque side to Sidári at the coves along the ✦ *Canal d'Amour,* where several low-lying rocky headlands project out to sea, some with caves below. The narrow strips of sand are no way large enough to accommodate the crowds of sun-worshippers who come here. Loungers spread out across the green hills, cliff terraces and the lawns in front of hotels and tavernas. For a spot of fun and action, hire a pedal boat or swim out to the off-shore rocky out-crops. You won't be alone here either, but the views are unique. ⬛ B2

8 ASTRAKÉRI
6km (3.7 miles) / 30 mins on bike from Róda.

Are you wary of eating fish, squid and calamari? Then head to the taverna *Gregóris (signposted | €€)* and give octopus a go. Whether you opt to have it grilled or braised, you won't find a better place to try this delicacy on the island. It's not only the octopus that makes it worth stopping here, the calamari taste vastly different from the chewy rings of rubber available back home, and the waiter will remove the bones before serving the freshly caught fish. Vassíli, the owner, usually waits on you in person and provides tips on how to best eat scampi if it's your first time. The traditional Corfiot *bourdétto* is on the daily menu. You can choose between boneless dogfish fil-lets or squid as its main ingredient. The langoustines are also affordable especially if Vassíli offers you Greek lobster, known as *kol-opída*, meaning "langoustines without antennae". To enjoy the full range of specialities and atmosphere, we recommend staying for both lunch and evening meal, and spend the time in between at the deserted sandy beach just 30m /100ft away. ⬛ B2

INSIDER TIP
Try some new seafood

9 STRINÍLAS
10km (6.2 miles) / 20 mins drive from Acharávi

Do you have a head for heights? Then take a trip that combines the highest mountain and the highest village on the island. Drive up the Pantokrátoras, followed by a break at the 🐗 *Taverna Oasis (daily | €)* on the tiny *platía* of this mountain village. The elm tree here is 200 years old, in whose shade you can escape the midday sun. ⬛ C3

10 NÍMFES
9km (5.6 miles) / 45 mins on bike from Acharávi

Like a puzzle? The *Naos Evstrámenou*, which is located on the outskirts of Nímfes is a unique construction, and continues to baffle historians. It has a dome similar to that of a Ceylonese *dagoba* – a form of Buddhist temple – which rises up over a hexagonal base. Is the shape a coincidence or was the church designed by a Corfiot sailor after his journeys around the Indian Ocean? A question to mull over while enjoying a sundowner later in the day. Meanwhile, if you have always wanted to know how kumquats are grown, then head to the village centre where you can see the fruit growing in a large valley plantation below the vil-lage square. The church on your left probably dates from the 18th century. *Left of the road from Plátonas to Nímfes (signposted)* ⬛ C3

11 PANTOKRÁTOR ★
18km (11 miles) / 40 mins drive from Nissáki

Once you have reached the top you can't get any higher on the island. At an altitude of 906m / 3,000ft, the view from the summit is breathtaking as it takes in the whole island and, on clear days, reaches as far as Albania and the Greek mainland. But don't be deceived: what often appears to be the boot of Italy in the distance is just a layer of mist! A tarmac road takes you up the mountain to the narrow car park on the mountain ridge, where it can be a hair-raising experience trying to turn your vehicle. Walk past a small café to reach the aptly-named monastery Pantokrátoras, which literally translates as "the Almighty", clearly a reference to Jesus Christ rather than the mountain itself. Since 1998, it has been occupied once again in the summer months – alternately by a priest from a nearby mountain village and a monk from a Corfiot monastery. Since then, time-consuming restoration of the church frescoes has taken place, and some of them have now regained their 17th-century splendour. The monastery is open every day to visitors. *D3*

12 PALEÓ PERÍTHIA ★

15km / 9.3 miles drive from Acharávi

Paleó Períthia looks like a museum village from the Venetian period. Situated in a fertile, high-altitude valley below Pantokrátor, it was quite well-off in the past, as can be seen by the large, sturdy stone houses and churches. However, its inhabitants moved down to the coast where they founded *Néa Períthia* (New Períthia). Only a few elderly shepherds remained.

The village fell into oblivion and so escaped the building boom of the 1970s and '80s. In the early 1990s, the first tavern opened and, today, there are four. The locals like the *Taverna*

At the summit of Pantokrátor is a small monastery with wonderful frescoes

It is only from the air that you can fully appreciate the double beach at Pórto Timióni

Fóros best – partly because of its excellent walnut cake. While there, ask the owner Thomas for a business card, he will draw you one in a matter of seconds!

INSIDER TIP
A true original

Buses only twice a day to Loútses, then 3km / 1.9 miles on foot 🗺 *D3*

🔟 AGÍA EKATERÍNI
8km (5 miles) / 30mins on bike from Archarávi

Pure wilderness! The north-east tip of Corfu is formed by the island of Agía Ekateríni which is covered in ferns and forests of pine, cypress and eucalyptus trees. There are no inhabitants here, even tavernas and beach bars are banned from the island. Bridges lead to the island; the one from Acharávi may only be used by pedestrians, cyclists and moped riders; the one to Ágios Spirídonas is also open to cars (even though not many people are aware of this).

On the mainland side, it is separated from the rest of Corfu by *Antoniótis*, a lake of brackish water that is rich in fish, and its two tributaries connecting it to the sea. The deserted *Agía Ekateríni* Monastery which dates from 1713, lies hidden in a small forest. Paths also lead off the main trail to small, almost deserted, shingle beaches where nude bathing is possible.

However, the 100-m / 328-ft-long *sandy beach* at 🏖 *Ágios Spirídonas* is much nicer; its gentle incline also makes it suitable for small children. There is a new, photogenic chapel right on the beach. *The Pyramid (corfupyramid.com)* is located 200m / 656ft away in the neighbouring bay, with its stylish beach club, mini golf course, playground and beach restaurant. 🗺 *C2*

ÁGIOS GEÓRGIOS & AROUND

(🗺 A3) **Four resorts all beginning with A and all guaranteeing a great holiday: Ágios Geórgios North, Arillás, Ágios Stéfanos are strung along the coast, while the inland village ★ Afiónas is perched on the mountain ridge and towers above the other three.**

All three coastal resorts, with their long stretches of sandy beaches, are a haven for sun worshippers. Although they have managed to ward off large hotel complexes and all-inclusive accommodation, the resorts are still vibrant places with a good selection of bars and tavernas.

The village of Afiónas offers an idyllic rural backdrop, with its excellent tavernas and delightful setting. From there, you can walk down to the beach of *Pórto Timióni* situated around two separate coves. This bay is not accessible by car or moped but still gets extremely busy at high season (and has no toilets...).

EATING & DRINKING

EVDAÍMON

No matter how often you go, you will never be disappointed with the standard of cooking in this restaurant. Jánnis from Corfu and Evangelía from Athens conjure up a new menu every day, using only the finest and freshest ingredients.

The split pea puree *fava*, originating from the island of Santorini, replaces the common-place *tzatziki* (which is after all readily available in supermarkets back home). All the sauces and dishes are homemade, with a generous addition of herbs.

This splendid cuisine is accompanied by amazing views, especially at sunset. *Daily from 1pm | Afiónas | on the main road | €€*

SHOPPING

CORFU BREWERY 🐷

A toast to Corfu and this, its brand new (and indeed only) brewery! This is a young venture in need of support. Guided tours are organised on Saturdays, and its shop is open six days a week selling eight different types of brews, beer glasses, etc. *Mon–Sat 9am–3pm, guided tours only Sat 10.30am–12.30pm | Arillás | next to the service station on the road to Magouládes*

ÍLIOS LIVING ART 🎏

The perfect place for the romantically minded and shell collectors. The jewellery designer Alex can cast things you have found or that have been washed up on the shore, in bronze, silver or gold for you to wear as a pendant in less than 40 minutes. *Ágios Geórgios Pagón | on the road to the beach | ilios-living-art.com*

OLIVES & MORE

This is where you can find first-class olive oil and products made from it, as well as creations conjured up by the

Paleokastrítsa and its neighbouring coastline is one of the most beautiful areas of Corfu

owners Heidi and Rainer themselves, who are often to be found sitting outside the shop on Afiónas's *platia*. Doing business almost seems a hobby to them, but they have been here for 20 years selling olive oil-based products including delicious pastes in stunningly decorated containers.

Heidi also teaches acrylic painting in four-hour-courses. *Sun–Fri 10am–2pm and 3–9pm, Sat only 3–9pm | Afiónas | at the top end of the village square*

SPORT & ACTIVITIES

Water-sports enthusiasts should head to *Sun & Fun Watersports (tel. 69 74 31 71 99 | sunfunclubcorfu .blogspot.com)* on the Ágios Geórgios beach in front of Hotel Alkyon. They have jet skis, water skis, canoes, paddle and motor boats for hire.

You can also take a taxi-boat to Timióni Beach which can otherwise only be reached on foot. There are donkey rides for kids from 5pm in Afiónas.

BEACHES

You can decide for yourself how much (or how little) you want to wear on the 2-km / 1.2-mile long beach between Arillás and Ágios Stéfanos, as long as you keep a discreet distance away from the resort's centre.

PALEO-KASTRÍTSA

(□ B4)) **When Corfiots are asked to name the most beautiful place on Corfu, most answer with Paleokastrítsa. In short, it is a place of superlatives and explains why most cruise-ship passengers head straight to the village after debarking from their luxury liners. They tend to have to make do with a quick glance from sea level, or – if they are a lucky – a quick dash up to the cliffs for a photo from above.**

When you arrive in Paleokastrítsa, you are likely to be left wondering where the actual village is. The road stretches 3km / 1.8 miles from the village entrance sign to the seafront, where it comes to an end. Except for a handful of hotels and shops and a few signs pointing to village tavernas, this appears to be it. There is no centre as such, and there never has been; the blanket of olive groves has always covered the sprinkling of houses so the small bays (ideal for swimming) as well as the port are hidden from sight. Even the village's most famous attraction, its monastery, cannot be spotted from the village.

The best way of exploring the true charm of Paleokastrítsa and its surrounding landscape is to take a boat ride or drive up to the mountain village of Lákones.

WELLNESS

This region has a number of organisations offering retreats in a range of disciplines, from yoga to meditation and pilates. All summer long, you can pack your bags, escape the high-season crowds and disappear for a few days' relaxation in the northern hills. *Alexiszorbas.com, manto-corfu.com*

NIGHTLIFE

The resort has many bars but none in particular are worth mentioning. Go where the party takes you or start one yourself, for example at *Ámmos* in Arillás, *Bar 38* in Ágios Stéfanos or *Dichtiá* in Ágios Geórgios.

SIGHTSEEING

BOAT TOUR

The whole day long, skippers stand waiting for visitors to arrive where the road ends at the large car park and the village's only traffic lights. They take guests on a 40-minute boat ride along the bay of Paleokastrítsa, which consists of many tiny coves. They sail up close to the sea caves and beaches, which can only be reached by boat, along the precipitous, green coastline and rugged cliffs on which the village's most famous monastery stands.

This area serves as a beach getaway perfect for outdoor enthusiasts, who most often hire a boat on their own in order to be able to pull in at the large number of isolated beaches.

PALEOKASTRÍTSA MONASTERY

It's ironic that almost nobody seriously considers life in a monastery nowadays yet crowds of people flock to visit this one every summer. To capture a halfway decent picture of the monastery's impressive location, walk past the monastery taverna and cemetery for five minutes along the seafront. From here, you will realise for the first time that the white monastery perches on a precipitous headland at the foot of some steep cliffs.

**INSIDER TIP
Get a better snap**

With its shady arcades, elegant arches, courtyard full of flowers and modest 18th-century buildings, the *Panagía Theotókou tis Paleokastrítsas* (monastery of "The Holy Bearer of God of Paleokastrítsa") is an idyllic location. The perfect photo of the monastery is complete if you manage to catch a shot of one of the three monks who still live there.

The paintings inside the church are reminiscent of a time without photography and in which paint served as the medium to record events. The church's most precious icon has been placed at the front on the left-hand wall. The work from 1653 only measures 43cm by 33cm and shows three Fathers of the Church, identifiable by their stoles decorated with crosses. Behind them, there is a depiction of a dramatic event that actually occurred on Corfu on the feast day of these three saints, on 30 January, in 1653. A firework that had been lit in their honour exploded while a nurse holding a child in her arms was standing nearby. As if by miracle, the child remained uninjured although the nurse was killed. She can be seen clearly in the right-hand section of the painting. Blood is pouring out of her side, she falls to the ground while still holding the child in her arms. The child's parents donated the icon as a sign of their gratitude to the saints for this miracle; the text to the right of the strip of pictures gives a detailed description of the occurrence.

There are two more icons at the back of the church on the left-hand and right-hand walls. They were painted in 1713 and illustrate four scenes of the Creation. The illustrations of animals are both cute and naïve. *April–Oct daily 7am–1pm and 3–8pm; the best time to visit is before 9am and after*

5pm when the hordes of tourists have left the church. Whatever you do, don't park in the spaces reserved for buses – the drivers will block you in mercilessly! | admission free

EATING & DRINKING

HORIZON

The splendid location of this taverna is hidden away from sight, as is so typical for Paleokastrítsa. Only by following the steps leading down from the road will you be treated to panoramic views of the magnificent bay. Great service, good food. *Daily | on the main road, next to Hotel Odysseus | Paleokastrítsa* | €€

SHOPPING

STREET MARKET

A row breaks out in the village every year between local market stallholders – who want to set up their stands as close to the monastery as possible to attract the buses full of tourists – and the local council – who would prefer to move them along to the drab car park at the traffic lights, hidden away from the cruise passengers. It's worth a look around just to see who has the upper hand in this dispute! There are a lot of African crafts for sale – a sign of Corfu's modern multiculturalism. Alongside is a range of local natural products and painted objects of all sorts. The pebbles painted with Corfiot motifs make nice little gifts or look good on your windowsill at home.

BEACHES

The pebbly beaches in the three large bays of *Ambeláki*, *Spíridon* and *Alípa* are easy to reach. Flights of steps lead down from the main road to other smaller pebbly bays. *Liapádes'* shingle beach is around 150 m / 492 ft long. None of them are really ideal for small

Tourist magnet: the romantic monastery of Panagía Theotókou tis Paleokastrítsas

Perfectly positioned on the top of a cliff: Angelókastro

children. Boat taxis leave from *Spíridon Beach*, the pier in front of the La Grotta Bar, the harbour at *Alípa Beach* and *Liapádes Beach* for the numerous other sandy and shingle bays that can only be reached from the sea.

NIGHTLIFE

LA GROTTA

For a spectacular setting and a heavy dose of kitsch, take the 142 steps leading down to the seafront, leaving reality behind you to enter a fantasy world with an artificial cave, rock faces lit up in colour, straw parasols and wooden walkways over the water. The local night owls here are, in fact, bats, and you can even spot fish diving out of the water. The sound of the waves is accompanied by soft background music. The ultimate place to chill out and maybe go for a night swim. *Daily* | *Paleokastrítsa*

AROUND PALEO- KASTRÍTSA

⑭ LÁKONES
5km (3.1 miles) / 15-min drive from Paleokastrítsa

The whole of Lákones is one large balcony. The village makes a living from its amazing view over Paleokastrítsa, the monastery and bays, and the steep coastline and green hills all around. Those who had or could borrow money, built cafés and tavernas commanding panoramic views; the main reason why people come here.

Visit *Castellino* (€€€), the region's highest restaurant, to try their homemade walnut cake, or *Café Dolce* (€), which serves an espresso you'd expect only in Italy. If you are looking for a wild time, join in the all-day parties of tour groups – mainly from Eastern Europe – around the pool at the *Golden Fox (€€)*, which always welcome new faces. All the pubs and restaurants are well-signposted from the village road. *⊞ B4*

15 MAKRÁDES

9km (5.6 miles) / 25-min drive from Paleokastrítsa

Makrádes (pop. 300) appears as a place from another time with its century-old houses and narrow lanes where no car dares to go. Nowhere else on Corfu has so many inhabitants that specialise in selling herbs and local table wine as here. Fierce competition forces them to make furious attempts to stop any passing car!

In the *Colombo* taverna *(daily | €)* in the village square, there is a 200-year-old olive press and you can sample many Corfiot specialities and all kinds of meat from the charcoal grill. *⊞ B4*

16 ANGELÓKASTRO ★

10km (6.2 miles) / 25-min drive from Paleokastrítsa

A race to the top! You can reach the castle from the car park in just five minutes, but most take ten minutes at a gentler pace. Whatever your speed, the views from the top will stop you in your tracks: the ruins of this Byzantine-Venetian "Angels' Castle" are a fascinating sight; they stand high above the west coast on a mountain peak with steep slopes on all sides. The panorama is just as breathtaking as the walk up.

Until the last Turkish invasion of the island in 1716, this fortification repeatedly offered refuge to the population of northern Corfu when enemies or pirates approached. Nobody was ever able to conquer Angelókastro.

A tarmac road takes you from Makrádesto Kriní, from where, it is just 700m / 2,296ft to the castle's car park, where there is a small taverna (€). You'll have to walk up a steep path for the last seven to ten minutes, but you will be rewarded with a wonderful view for your effort. *Freely accessible out of season, in the summer daily 8am–7pm | admission 2 euros | ⊞ B4*

THE SOUTH

Although less spectacular than the island's dramatic north, Corfu's south still has its own special charm, with a lake, two photogenic river harbours, a magical forest and miles of sandy beaches with dunes and steep cliffs. Glow worms can be spotted in summer, and pink flamingos are a special treat for tourists who arrive early on or very late in the year. The roads are far less winding than in the north, and you feel less rushed to cram in all the sights.

View over Chlómos

The majority of the large hotels run by travel operators line the coast between Benítses and Messongí, with one in Ágios Górdis and one near Lefkími. Most other tourists stay in small guesthouses and apartments where the evening's entertainment is provided by a handful of tavernas and bars. The advantage (or maybe disadvantage) is you are guaranteed to bump into someone you met the night before.

THE SOUTH

Ágios Górdis
p. 86

Ágios Górdis Beach

1 Pendáti

Benítses 7

27km, 45 mins

Δαφνάτα
Dafnata

Κάτω Παυλιάνα
Kato Pavliana

Κορνάτα
Kornata

Βουνιατάδες
Vouniatades

19km, 30 mins

Στρογγυλή
Stroggili

2 Paramónas

Επισκοπιανά
Episkopiana

Άγιος Ματθαίος
Ágios Mattheos

Moraítika
p. 88

Messongí
p. 88

8 Gardíki

3 Vraganiotika

Χαλικούνας
Chalikoúnas

Άγιος Δημήτριος
Ágios Dimitrios

Boúkari 5

Alonáki ★

Χλοματιανά
Chlomatiana

Chlómos ★ 4

Chalikoúnas Beach

GREECE
ΕΛΛΑΔΑ

Kérkyra
(Korfu)

Limni
Korission

Issos Beach

Αργυρό
Argira

Ágios Geórgios South ★
p. 92

Ionio Pelagos

2 km
1.24 mi

MARCO POLO HIGHLIGHTS

★ **CHLÓMOS**
The south's most beautiful mountain village ➤ p. 90

★ **ÁGIOS GEÓRGIOS SOUTH**
Sand and dunes like nowhere else on the island ➤ p. 92

★ **ALONÁKI**
Good food in a wonderful garden setting in Chalikúnas ➤ p. 93

★ **LEFKÍMI**
Corfu's prettiest river port ➤ p. 94

Ionio Pelagos

Κορακάδες
Korakades

Petriti 6 ☀

Nótos Beach
Νότος
Nótos

Άγιος Νικόλαος
Ágios Nikolaos

Μαραθιάς
Marathias

Περιβόλι
Perivoli

9 **Lefkími** ★

Βιταλάδες
Vitalades

14km, 20 mins 🚗

Κρητικά
Kritika

Νεοχώρι
Neochori

Δραγωτινά
Dragotina

10 **Kávos**

Παλαιοχώρι
Paleochori

Σπαρτερά
Spartera

Always in sight of the sea: at Plóri tavern in Paramónas you can dine at the water's edge

ÁGIOS GÓRDIS

(🗺 C6) **At the south end of Ágios Górdis, a rocky pinnacle rises out of the water like an exclamation mark indicating the beguiling beauty of this long stretch of beach. Striking rock formations on the surrounding cliffs soar up to provide the perfect backdrop for a romantic sunset.**

A blemish on this pristine landscape is the Pink Palace – the work of an ambitious hotelier that would fit in better in Barbie's world than on Corfu's coastline. But the building does little to spoil the mood of this tiny resort geared to holidaymakers; just 200m / 650ft long, its main street is bursting with good bars and tavernas on both sides and you will not find a more compact, lively nightlife scene anywhere else on the island.

EATING & DRINKING

ARK KITCHEN BAR

This casually designed beach bar is the perfect place if you don't plan to move around much on holiday. Have breakfast here before heading to the beach (with free sun loungers and parasols for local guests), followed by a snack for lunch, an ice cream later on in the afternoon and an evening meal for sunset. It also hosts live music and rock. If things get wild, you can even spend the night on the beach. *Daily from 9am | in the southern section of the beach | €€*

LINDA'S

Woven backrest chairs, white tablecloths and flowers on the tables – the proprietor Sophia knows what her guests expect. Plates are garnished with sprigs of rosemary, vine leaves and onion rings as a sign of her good taste. Corfiot specialities, such as *sofríto,* are definitely worth trying here.

Daily, evenings only | on the main road to the beach | €€

SPORT & ACTIVITIES

All the usual water sports are on offer on the beach here. However, those

INSIDER TIP
Give gliding a go

seeking new thrills can also try out tandem paragliding, which is on offer from *Activetours (tel. 69 41 41 58 01 | costs around 90 euros | corfuparagliding.gr).* It's not for the faint-hearted, but those brave enough to give it a go will – if the wind is blowing in the right direction (and fortunately it usually is) – be taken up to heights of 400m / 1,300ft by an experienced pilot and then glide along the striking southern coast for up to 20 minutes.

BEACHES

Ágios Górdis's sandy beach stretches for over a kilometre (half a mile). There are loungers and parasols to hire all along it.

NIGHTLIFE

LEMON TREE
Forget yellow; the favourite colours of the proprietors of this trendy cocktail bar are undoubtedly lilac and violet. Run by a family of four, consisting of three bearded brothers, Thános, Michális and Geórgios, and their long-haired sister, Samantha, this open-air bar serves cocktails with a unique colour and taste. Underneath the shade of the large lemon tree, guests can sit

on cosy wooden benches – the more sociable alternative to the bar stools elsewhere – and discuss the difference between lilac and violet... *Daily from 6pm | north of the village road*

MIKE'S DANCING PUB
Fed up with sitting outside? The resort's only indoor bar gets busy around 10pm, hosting live acts, karaoke every Wednesday and even Beatles revival shows. Music from the '80s fits the retro vibe of this pub. *Daily from 10pm | at the junction bus stop*

AROUND ÁGIOS GÓRDIS

🔟 PENDÁTI
11km (6.8 miles) / 20-min drive from Ágios Górdis; only 2km / 1.2 miles on foot
If you stay in Ágios Górdis, you should take the 20–30-minute walk up to the unspoiled mountain village of Pendáti at least once. The path winds up the steep coastline through dense green fields, offering contrasting views of the rocky headland and the beach. Drivers can also enjoy the breath-taking panorama over Ágios Górdis from the two terraces at *Chris Place (€).* Owner Sofía prepares a freshly made moussaká every day – it's best at lunchtime! *C–D6*

INSIDER TIP
The best moussaká

2 PARAMÓNAS
13km (8.1 miles) / 25-min drive from Ágios Górdis

If a 300-m / 984-ft-long beach with only 30 parasols, sounds like your idea of idyllic seclusion, Paramónas is the place for you. This tiny hamlet is made up of just 12 houses, each with a large garden to guarantee some respectful distance from its neighbours. To say it is peaceful here would be an understatement. The taverns *Plóri (€)* and *Sun Set (€)* are, however, both of a good standard and right on the coast, and – as the latter's name implies – you're best to get a table (at either of them) as the sun begins its descent. *D7*

MESSONGÍ & MORAÍTIKA

(D7) **A tiny passenger ferry and a wide road bridge link the coastal resorts of Messongí (pop. 290) and Moraítika (pop. 600). A small river, which empties into the sea in summer, separates the two. If you are after evocative images of Corfu, you can do a lot worse than the group of fishing and excursion boats that moor at the port of Messongí by the river's mouth.**

Otherwise, the villages offer little for tourists. Situated to the south of the river, *Messongí* consists of a row of houses between the promenade and narrow sandy-pebbly beach.

The more modern part of *Moraítika* is divided between a wider stretch of beach lined with hotels and simple beach bars and the busy main road dotted with supermarkets, bars and restaurants. A far more picturesque destination awaits you in the old village of *Moraítika* on the hill behind the main road, with its small choice of pretty tavernas.

EATING & DRINKING

BACCHUS 🐖
Small, discreet taverna with a shady, leaf-covered veranda, polyglot proprietor and spotless dining area. Freshly made regional cooking and excellent value for money. *Daily, evenings only | at the southern end of Messongí's beach | bacchus.gr | €*

OLD VILLAGE TAVERNA
This taverna with a flower-adorned terrace is located directly on the tiny village square of old Moraítika. The landlord Níkos takes pleasure in explaining, in various languages, the Corfiot dishes, which his wife prepares and his daughters often serve. *Daily from 6pm | €*

ZAKS
Chef Zacharías learned his trade in Bern and London. His experience in international gourmet cuisine and gastronomy is clearly evident in this fine-dining restaurant with excellent, yet not pretentious, service and a delicious menu. His waiters know how to flambé. Zacharías is no beginner when it comes to vegetarian cooking,

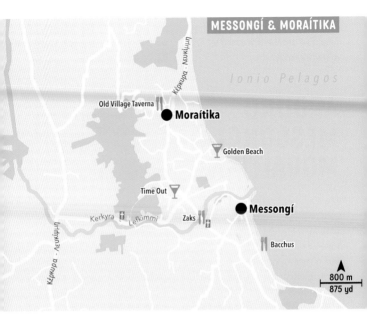

MESSONGÍ & MORAÍTIKA

Ionio Pelagos

Κέρκυρα - Λευκίμμη

Old Village Taverna — ● **Moraítika**

Golden Beach

Time Out

Kerkyra — Lefkimmi — Zaks

● **Messongí**

Bacchus

Κέρκυρα - Λευκίμμη

800 m
875 yd

ever since he cooked a dinner for Prince Charles in London. *Daily, evenings only | on the main road near the bridge | €€€*

SPORT & ACTIVITIES

There is a water-sports centre on the public beach in front of the Messongí Beach hotel, where you can hire canoes and pedalos or give water-skiing and parasailing a try.

BEACHES

As everywhere else on the east coast, the beaches at Messongí and Moraítika are very narrow and made up of coarse sand and pebbles. Both beaches get extremely crowded during the high season.

NIGHTLIFE

GOLDEN BEACH ⚑

Chrístos, the proprietor here, would be a serious contender for *The X Factor*. He is a lively (and multilingual) entertainer, hosting a different show every evening in summer. Whether it's Elvis shows, *syrtáki*, Latin nights or quiz evenings, Chrístos gets every guest to join in. The audience comes from all over Europe, making the evenings truly memorable. *Shows daily from about 8.30pm | on Moraítika beach*

TIME OUT

Not in a party mood? Relax and unwind from all the partying with some shisha in this small bar. Non-smoker? Then try one of the cocktails such as the Greek Doctor. Decide for yourself if one's enough, or if you need two or three to hit the spot. *On Moraítika's main street*

AROUND MESSONGÍ & MORAÍTIKA

🖪 VRAGANIOTIKA
3km (1.9 miles) / 5-min drive from Messongí-Moraítika

How is oil extracted from the olives? This question and more are answered on a guided tour of the *Olive Oil Factory* owned by Spíros and Vangélis Mavroúdis. Built in 1993, the factory houses ultra-modern equipment. In contrast, the open-air museum next door shows visitors how difficult it was to extract the oil in the past. You can try and, of course, buy all the oils at the end of the tour. *(Mon–Sat 8.30am–8pm, Sun 9am–1pm | admission free | on the main road in the direction of Lefkími).* Just outside the village, there are two restaurants that are definitely worth trying. The first, *Archontiko (daily | Chlomatiana | tel. 26 61 07 58 51 | Facebook: archontiko-corfu | €€€)* has glorious views down to the coast from its hill-top setting; its excellent steaks have become a local favourite for Corfiots and tourists alike. The second is the secluded rural *Bioporos* taverna *(daily | follow signs from the village high street for 1.5km / 1 mile along a dirt track | tel. 26 61 07 62 24 |* *bioporos.gr | €),* Corfu's only exclusively organic restaurant; it not only has delicious dishes using lots of produce from its own farm, but also has a good range of natural and organic wines and spirits – including a delicious *tsipouro* brandy. *▭ D7*

> **INSIDER TIP**
> **Organic farm and restaurant**

🖪 CHLÓMOS ★
4km (2.5 miles) / 10–15-min drive from Messongí-Moraítika

If the north's cup runneth over with beautiful mountain villages, the south's glass looks decidedly less than half empty. Chlómos is, however, the exception that proves the rule. In theatre-like rows, the homes of its 700 inhabitants stick out against an otherwise lush green landscape and are linked to each by a network of narrow alleyways and flights of stairs. Out of season, the village is, sadly largely empty. Praise be to Zeus then for the two fine tavernas that bring visitors in every day – one at each end of the village. Both have something to offer: in the south, *Sirtaki (daily | €)* has a glorious view over the village, whereas in the north *Balis (daily | €)* has the better food and great views down to the coast and the sea. *▭ E7*

🖪 BOÚKARI
6km (3.7 miles) / a good 90-min walk from Messongí-Moraítika

For a long time, the small fishing port of Boúkari (pop. 50) was home to just one fish taverna: *Karídis (daily | €€€).* The eatery was so good that it attracted more and more guests, including

Paradise in the Panórama garden – delicious food, and a hammock for relaxing in

celebrities. Others followed suit, and today there are over half a dozen good fish tavernas well-spaced along the road between the port and Messongí. Each of them has established a loyal following, but if you want to try the traditional *bourdetto* soup, Karidis has yet to be surpassed; you can pick the fish you want from the restaurant's fridge yourself and then choose how spicy you want the dish (white for mild, red for a bit of a kick). *E7*

6 PETRÍTI

15km (9.3 miles) / 30-min drive from Messongí-Moraïtika

Why do Egyptians come to Corfu? For a holiday if they are millionaires, or to be hired as fishermen if they are struggling to survive back home. They work on the large fishing boats, like the ones you see daily in the port of Petrití, carefully mending the fishing nets.

Their catch of the day is then served in the fish tavernas along the port. Petrití mainly attracts independent travellers, which is not a bad thing.

The village's own beach is far less attractive than the sandy *Nótos Beach,* which is 70m / 230ft long and lies on the other side of the rocky island at the south end of the village. If you don't enjoy sand, spend a relaxing day in the 🍴 garden of the *Panórama* taverna *(tel. 26 62 05 17 07 | panoramacorfu.gr | €€)* on the other side of the headland. Surrounded by banana plants and blossoming shrubs, yucca palms and flowers, you can lie back and relax on the sun loungers and beach chairs dotted around the garden. There is also a wooden jetty to help bathers access the water. The owners, Thanássis Vagiás and his wife Ina, prepare deliciously aromatic Greek specialities, making it even more difficult to prise yourself away from this idyllic spot. If you don't want to leave, the family also rents 15 spacious apartments in the middle of olive groves about 150m / 360ft away from the taverna. *E7*

7 BENÍTSES
18km (23 miles) / 25-min drive from Ágios Geórgios South
Proximity to the airport once made Bentíses one of Corfu's main resorts, and its many large hotels means it often crops up in travel agents' catalogues. Apart from its proximity to the city, there is however little to recommend this corner of the island. It does boast a few scant remains of small Roman baths from the second century CE in the centre of the old village, but even its beaches are always too packed for them to be much fun. *D6*

ÁGIOS GEÓRGIOS SOUTH

(D–E8) **Some beaches just resemble one large sand pit – not so ★ Ágios Geórgios South, whose official name is Ágios Geórgios Argirádon. There is enough space here for everyone, whether they want to lie back and bask in the sun or to play games and party. Issos Beach is a sunbather's paradise with no shady spots; it is also relatively unspoilt by modern mass tourism.**

A miniature desert-like dune landscape starts where all the roads end directly on the northern edge of the resort. The dunes stretch as far as Corfu's largest inland lake, at whose end a narrow 5-km / 3-mile-long spit stretches out between the brackish lake and the sea beyond. This is a tranquil spot for anyone seeking peace and quiet. For the more adventurous, a surf, standup paddle and kite station is situated at the northern end of the spit. Those looking for a little evening entertainment should head to Ágios Geórgios's 2-km / 1.2-mile-long promenade (at whose southern end begins another long stretch of beach).

SIGHTSEEING

LAKE KORÍSSION
If you come from a country with plenty of lakes, you might well scoff at Lake Koríssion, but the Corfiots are very proud of it largely because it is the only inland lake on the island. A thin strip of sand and dunes separates the

A narrow strip of land separates Lake Koríssion from the sea

lake from the sea, with just one small gap along the 5-km / 3-mile shore to allow a small stream of water to flow into the Mediterranean. This channel is almost exactly at the halfway point between Ágios Geórgios in the south and the tiny village of Chalikoúnas in the north and can be crossed by a footbridge.

If you cross the bridge and keep going, you will eventually reach the water-sports station at the other end of the lake. Keep going a little bit further to find the small sandy bay at *Alonáki:* ✦ *Chalikoúnas beach,* home to one of the island's best tavernas. Both the taverna and water-sports station can be reached by car, although the way is not that easy to find. *D7–8*

EATING & DRINKING

ALONÁKI ★ ⚑

Apricots and figs almost fall straight into your mouth, while cats crave your attention and swallows flit in and out of their nests under the terrace. Inside,

you will find a wonderful oasis from the baking Corfiot heat. All in all, it's not far off paradise – and that's before we have even got to the food. The inn-keeper's family serves delicacies, including *lachanodolmádes* (stuffed cabbage leaves), rabbit *stifádo*, and a real *skórpios bourdétto* with scorpion-fish – they are absolutely delicious with a real "zing" in their tails . *Daily | well signposted from the road to Chalikoúnas beach | €*

O KAFÉSAS

In the most unusual taverna in Ágios Geórgios, you sit on terraces above a little-used road with a view of the sea. Ákis, the proprietor, has decorated the taverna tastefully. The bread comes straight out of the clay oven; the vegetables, olive oil and chickens are from his farm, and the fish is home-smoked. The mixed pickles – *toursí* – are in a league of their own and the *bourdétto* is made with stingray. There is usually live Greek music on Saturday evenings. *Daily | on the coast road in the south village | €€*

Mending fishing nets can be monotonous work, but fun in the right company

SPORT & ACTIVITIES

Ágios Geórgios South is the best place for windsurfing, and the only resort on the island to offer kite surfing. The latest trend is stand-up paddleboarding, and guided tours are organised by *Kite Club Corfu (tel. 69 77 14 56 14 | kite-club-corfu.com)* at Chalikoúnas beach to the north of the spit; for more information on all these activities, go to the *Harley* café at the northern end of the promenade.

NIGHTLIFE

HARLEY

This cafe is open all day, and develops into a lively meeting place for surfers in the evening. This is where they not only talk shop and listen to good music, but also play *távli* and KoJa golf – a kind of miniature golf developed by the owners, Bavaria-born Anita and her Greek husband Jánnis. *Daily | at the northern end of the coastal road*

AROUNND ÁGIOS GEÓRGIOS SOUTH

8 GARDÍKI

13km / 8.1 miles from Ágios Geórgios South

This 13th-century Byzantine castle, with its octagonal defence wall and towers of quarried stone and rows of brick, is the most important historical site in the southern part of the island. Due to danger of collapse, going inside is strictly forbidden. *D7*

9 LEFKÍMI ★

16km (9.9 miles) / 25-min drive from Ágios Geórgios South

Despite being the largest town in the south (pop. 3,500), Lefkími has remained almost untouched by tourism. Accommodation is scarce and there is only a handful of tavernas and one popular café along its riverbanks.

One kilometre away from the town, the River Chimarós flows into the sea next to a beautiful sandy beach, which has only one snack bar and no water activities to offer. The river was once the town's port, housing small warehouses and workshops; today it is the town's most photogenic attraction.

Provided you have a good zoom function on your camera, another sight worth capturing is the hundreds of pink flamingos which flock to the former saltworks at *Alikés* every year between October and May. The shore here is extremely flat and makes for great swimming, especially for small children. The only taverna along the shore rents out a handful of parasols and sun loungers. ▯ F8

INSIDER TIP
One-legged wonders

🔟 KÁVOS

22km / 13.7 miles from Ágios Geórgios South

The island's most southerly town is the place where Brits come to party on Corfu. The beach is narrow and over-run with young people while the main street is more crowded at 4am than 4pm. By sunrise, the street is covered in broken bottles and drunken teenagers trying to find their way back to their hotel. What else can you expect when the shots are handed out for less than a euro? *kavosnightlife. com* | ▯ G8

STAY ON THE SEASHORE

Lots of hotels claim to be "right on the beach", but *Christina Beach* means it. From its ground-floor rooms, the sea is no more than 20 steps from your bed. The only downside is that the owner, Dimitri, requires a minimum stay of three nights. It could be worse... *16 rooms | Messongi | can be reached from the shore road| Tel: 26 61 07 67 71 | hotelchristina.gr | €€ | ▯ D7*

THERE IS ANOTHER WAY

If you are looking for a place to leave the rest of the world behind... look no further. *Alonáki* guesthouse offers simple accommodation in rooms (optionally with kitchen facilities – for 5 euros extra) and is far away from any other hotel. Corfiot food is served in the guesthouse's garden taverna. There is a tiny sandy beach right in front of the house. Another unspoilt beach is situated just ten minutes away with just two beach bars and one watersports station, that's it. The owner Katarína warmly welcomes guests and the rest of the family speak good English. *Ágios Geórgios South | tel. 26 61 07 58 72 | Facebook: alonaki-bay | € | ▯ D–E*

CENTRAL CORFU

PLENTY OF BEACHES IN EASY REACH OF THE TOWN

Are you the kind of have-your-cake-and-eat-it city person who wants a beach holiday but can't survive more than a few days outside the nearest metropolis? Then central Corfu is the perfect destination for you. From early morning to late evening, affordable bus services run between nearly all the resorts and the island capital, even a taxi will not cost you the earth.

Most of the island's large hotels are located in the broad bay between Kérkyra and Dassiá. But, only the birds see that. Even the

Mirtiótissa Beach

biggest complexes are well hidden in lush greenery, or separated from each other by gently rolling hills or coastal bays. Here, you will be able to spend your holidays in park-like surroundings on the seashore. Most of the beaches are narrow and usually pebbly, but the hotels offset this with spacious, beautiful sunbathing lawns and pool terraces. The sheltered bays are particularly attractive for water-skiing and paragliding. The beaches slope gradually into the water, so many hotels have built wooden jetties that can be used for sunbathing; if you want to take a swim, ladders make it easier to

CENTRAL CORFU

Ζυγός
Zygos

Σπαρτ
Spa

Άγιος Μάρκος
Ágios Markos

Αρκαδάδες
Arkadades

Σοκράκι **3**
Sokráki

2 Άνω Κορακιανά
Áno Korakianá

Κάτω Άγιος Μάρκος
Kato Ágios Markos

Ίψος
Ípsos

Αλειμματάδες
Alimatades

Σκριπερό
Skripero

Δουκάδες
Doukades

Κάτω Κορακιάνα
Kato Korakiana

Γαρδελάδες
Gardelades

Dassiá
p. 102

Λιαπάδες
Liapades

GREECE
ΕΛΛΑΔΑ

26km, 45 mins

Κανακάδες
Kanakades

Gou
p. 10

Τεμπλόνι
Temploni

Μάρμαρο
Marmaro

Κυρά Χρυσικό
Kira Chrisiko

Γιαννάδες
Giannades

Κουραμαδίτικα
Kouramaditika

4 Ropa Valley

Έρμονες **5**

Βάτος
Vatos

Mirtiótissa
p. 107

Sandy beach at Mirtiótissa ★

Kaiser's Thron

Glifáda Beach

Pélekas
p. 107

Glifáda
p. 107

Pélekas Beach

Yaliskári Beach

Sin

▲
2 km
1.24 mi

Νησσάκι
Nissaki

Μπαρμπάτι
Barbati

MARCO POLO HIGHLIGHTS

★ **IPAPÁNTI CHURCH**
A little known photogenic gem ➤ p. 102

★ **KAISER'S THRONE**
A majestic place to watch the sun set ➤ p. 107

★ **SANDY BEACH AT MIRTIÓTISSA**
Swim like you are in the Garden of Eden ➤ p. 109

★ **FOLKLORE MUSEUM**
See how Corfiots used to live ➤ p. 111

I o n i o

P e l a g o s

13km, 25 mins

Dafníla
p. 102

Ipapánti Church ★

Πτηχία (Βηδός)
Ptichia (Vidos)

● **Kontokáli**
p. 100

Αλυκές Ποταμού
Alykes Potamou

Εβροπούλοι
Evropouli

Ποταμός
Potamos

Μαντούκι
Mantouki

Κέρκυρα
Kérkyra (Korfu)

φρα
Afra

Αλεπού
Alepou

γιος Ιωάννης
gios Ioannis

K é r k y r a
(K o r f u)

Κομπίτσι
Kompitsi

13km, 25 mins

Κανόνι
Kanóni

Καστανιά
Kastania

Χρυσηίδα
Chrisiida

αρυπατάδες
rypatades

Καλαφατιώνες
Kalafationes

Σουλαίικα
Souleika

ραμάδες
uramades

Άγιος Προκόπιος
Ágios Prokopios

Folklore Museum ★

It's been a long time since ships were built here: the Venetian shipyards in Gouviá

GOUVIÁ & KONTOKÁLI

(□□ C–D 4) **There is probably no better image of the inequalities in wealth in modern Greece than the 960 luxury yachts in the marina at Gouviá (pop. 950), whose combined valued would easily exceed the GDP of some developing countries.**

The marina is open to the public, so visitors can get a closer look at all that money can buy you on the Mediterranean. Things have not changed since Venetian times: in the late 18th century, wealthy northern Italians would bring their galleons to be repaired and housed over winter in the old Venetian shipyards. The ships were not powered by sails but by slaves, who proved far more reliable than the wind. The wind is still a rare guest in *Kontokáli* (pop. 1,600).

SIGHTSEEING

VENETIAN SHIPYARDS

Today, the walls, arches and entrance portal of the shipyard, constructed in 1778, seem out of place and rather neglected – however, these buildings, which are now in ruins, were full of life in the last 20 years of Venetian dominance over Corfu. This is where ships were built, repaired and put into dry dock over winter. *Free access | between the main beach and marina, well signposted in the village ("Venetian shipyards")*

EATING & DRINKING

ROÚLA

Celebrities like to head off to far-flung places away from the madding crowds. Rather than idyllic spots, they are simply looking for somewhere to escape their hectic lives. And Roúla ticks all of these boxes. Located on an inlet off the bay, with views over the yacht harbour and mountains, this large fish taverna lies far away from any tourist centre. Workers are busy in the shipyards on the opposite side of the bay. Mikhail Gorbachev, Nana Mouskouri, Vicky Leandros and many other VIPs did not come here to swim (the water does not look especially inviting) but for the excellent fish and seafood. *Daily, evenings only; Sat & Sun also open for lunch | on the same peninsula as the Hotel Kontokáli Bay that is signposted on the main road | €€€*

TÁKIS

Many of the guests find the restaurant proprietor eccentric yet not unfriendly. He has original ideas which he likes to incorporate into his menu. The favourites are grilled dishes, but regulars go for his home-smoked trout from the Greek mainland and his rabbit is almost as good, if not better than the *kokorétsi*, grilled lamb offal wrapped in natural casing and

INSIDER TIP
Smoked fishy treats

grilled on the spit. *Daily; usually closed in the afternoon in July and August | €€*

SPORT & ACTIVITIES

There is a range of water sports – including pedalos, canoes, water-skiing, wakeboarding, banana-boating and paragliding – on offer from a company called *Corcyra Beach (tel. 69 77 33 46 32 | Corcyra-watersports.com)*. They are based next to the hotel of the same name. You will find many of the same activities on offer from *Kontokali Bay Watersports (tel. 69 77 22 43 14 | Facebook: kbwatersports)*, whose office is also located next to a hotel that shares their name.

BEACHES

The most beautiful beach in *Kontokáli* is located directly in front of the Hotel Kontokáli Bay and, like all other beaches in Greece, is open to the public. All of the other beaches between Kontokáli and *Gouviá* were sacrificed for the construction of the marina. Gouviá now only has a 200-m / 656-ft-long main beach and a strip beneath the Louis Corcyra Beach Hotel; both are mostly pebbly.

NIGHTLIFE

O2

This place isn't exactly going to take your breath away, but it is the coolest bar in the resort. *Daily | village road in the direction of Kontokáli*

DAFNÍLA & DASSIÁ

(□ C4) **The Club Med in the north of the green bay of Dassiá finally closed its doors in 2002. Today, it's hard to imagine that there were once crowds of affluent French tourists who spent their holidays on this peninsula for over 50 years. Perhaps even more unbelievably, they stayed in Polynesian-style huts, walked around half-naked and paid for food and drinks with glass beads. When the resort was set up, the journey to get here took two and a half days from Paris, with a stop in Venice!**

The larger Dafníla peninsula on the other side of the bay has since evolved into an exclusive holiday resort for the wealthy. Even the Russian billionaire Roman Abramovich has bought an estate there. The northern part of the peninsula today resembles a jungle dotted with the remains of straw huts.

Situated between the two extremes is the resort of *Dassiá* which has remained relatively normal. The island's main road cuts directly through the centre, leaving behind an uninspiring thoroughfare lined with bars and shops. A nicer place to spend the evening is at the beach with its lively beach bars and tavernas.

SIGHTSEEING

IPAPÁNTI CHURCH ★

Many couples tie the knot in this quaint church on the tiny island, and it is not just because of its romantic setting surrounded by cacti, agaves and flowers. The resident priest is very friendly and allows guests to use the surrounding gardens for the wedding celebrations afterwards – so attractive are they that guests hardly have time to talk to each other in between taking snaps. Even if you are not attending a wedding, it's worth taking the detour from the main road to visit this church (built in 1713). *Daily from noon | follow the small signpost to Koméno on the main island road*

EATING & DRINKING

DASSIÁ BEACH

If you were to look up "ideal beachside lunch spot" online, you might well get a photo of the Dassia Beach Hotel's terrace. Under the shade of beautiful trees, you can get high-quality Greek dishes at affordable prices. There is a dress code in the evening, but during the day there is no need to change out of your swimming costume. *Daily from 8am | in the middle of the beach | €*

ETRUSCO

Gastronomic guides describe Ettore Botrini's restaurant as the "avant-garde of Greek gastronomy", the best restaurant on any Greek island and the second best in the whole country. He is a disciple of the revolutionary "technomotion" style developed by Spain's star chef Andoni Luis Aduriz: he does not sell food but emotions; he doesn't nourish the stomach but the soul. The menu changes often and has offered such delicacies as medallions of fish in triple-sec with sesame, lamb simmered with kumquats and olive oil, and tomato ice cream. In spite of his fame, set meals are available from as little as 60 euros. *May–Oct; daily, evenings only | on the road from Dassiá to Áno Korakianá | tel. 26 61 09 33 42 | €€€*

KARIDIÁ

If you prefer a more down-to-earth Greek taverna which doesn't cost the earth, try the "walnut tree" restaurant. Surrounded by a splendid landscape,

you can sit on the veranda and be served Greek dishes and tasty salads freshly prepared every day by the owner's family. The house wine is pleasant and most of the vegetables come from their own gardens; vegetarians will love it here. *Daily, evenings only | Dassiá | on the main road | €€*

LEÓNIDAS GRILL ROOM 🐖

If you want to know where Corfiots go to eat, have a look at which restaurants stay open all year round. In Dassiá, Leónidas is the only one. Its following mainly comes from its excellent *gyros*

Picturesquely surrounded by water: the small church in Ipapánti in the south of Dafníla

and *souvláki*, but the sausages and lamb chops are also well worth trying. *Tue–Sun 5pm–2am | on the northern end of the main road | €*

MALIBU BEACH CLUB

This beach club caters to avid sun worshippers, serving snacks (ranging from toast to grilled octopus) to the sun loungers on the beach, lawn or at the poolside. A glass of champagne can also be ordered to accompany the evening sunset. *Daily | between the Ikos resorts | €*

SPORT & ACTIVITIES

There are three good water-sports centres on the main beach in Dassiá, with two others on the hotel beaches at Daphníla Bay and the Corfu Imperial.

INSIDER TIP
Up for a mini-cruise?

If you want to go out for a cruise on a boat, there are regular departures from the quay in the front of the Dassiá Beach Hotel. If you go for a whole day, the small boats will take you all the way up to Kassiópi; in a half day you can get down to Corfu Town.

BEACHES

The only beach worth mentioning on the Komméno Peninsula occupied by Dafníla is near the Hotel Corfu Imperial – the others are only really only worth going to if you are desperate for a dip. The main, mostly pebbly beach at Dassiá is around 700m / 2,296ft long. There is no beach road to disturb you while you swim in the midst of verdant nature. To make it easier to get in, you can jump into the water from static platforms. The quiet *Ágios Nikólaos Beach* between Dassiá and Dafníla has a 300-m / 984-ft stretch of sand. It is also the site of the – easily recognisable – country estate of the Russian oligarch Roman Abramovich, one of the world's richest men. There are often two large motor yachts anchored in front of his high-security residence.

NIGHTLIFE

EDEM BEACH NIGHTCLUB

Full moon or underground parties, retro sounds from the 1960s to 1990s and rock: there is always something going on between the end of May and September at one of the island's oldest beach clubs. "Party until you drop" is the motto here. Admission is free and if temperatures get too hot, you can cool down in the sea, which is just a stone's throw away. *Daily | Dassiá | in front of the Hotel Schería, approx. 100m / 328ft north of the Eléa Beach hotel*

TARTAYA

Lit up in colour and wrapped in colourful fabrics, the palm trees in this exotic lounge bar come in every shade ... except green. Only Ikea has a wider choice of lounge furniture and seating. If you partying alone, you can make yourself comfortable on one of the high stools at the bar. The resident DJ plays all the latest sounds. *Daily | Dassiá | on the main road north of the Chandris Hotel*

Sun loungers at the ready on Dassiá beachfront

AROUND DAFNÍLA & DASSIÁ

❶ ÍPSOS & PIRGI

2km (1.2 mile) / 5 mins by bus from Dafníla

Each to their own... Some holiday-makers may enjoy sunning themselves on the narrow strip of shingle directly below the busy main island road. After a hard day blocking out the traffic noise here, they may even enjoy crossing the road to an assortment of mediocre bars, restaurants, souvenir shops and campsites. As we say – each to their own. 🕮 *C4*

❷ ÁNO KORAKIÁNA

5km (3 miles) / 10–15-min drive from Dafníla

If you want to experience authentic village life untouched by tourism, then head to the large inland villages of Áno and Káto – Upper and Lower – Korakianá, with their 2,000 inhabitants and 37 (usually closed) churches and chapels. Visit the villages in the late afternoon from 5.30pm onwards, which is when the Venetian houses and narrow lanes come to life. Once the temperatures have begun to cool, children come out to play, teenagers gather on the streets and women sit gossiping in front of their houses while their men go off to play cards in the local *kafenío*. The sculptor Aristidis Metallinós (1908–87) is not part of this anymore.

The church and taverna are at the heart of every Corfiot village: evening in Pélekas

He once frequented these streets and even owned a nice museum on the main street of Áno Korakiána. Unfortunately, he didn't leave behind enough money for a curator, which is why the museum is now closed. Some of his works can, however, still be seen hanging on the walls and the roof of the museum.

In contrast, the *Aléxandros-Soútzos-Museum (Mon, Wed, Thu, Sat, Sun 8.30am–3.30pm, Wed, Fri 10am–2pm and 6–9pm | admission 2 euros | corfu. nationalgallery.gr)* in Káto Korakianáis is open on a regular basis. It belongs to the Greek National Gallery in Athens and exhibits some spectacular Greek art from the 18th century to today. The museum is housed in a medieval building with tower and was once a noble guesthouse and

subsequently a hotel. The likes of Kaiser Wilhelm II, Greek kings, the billionaire shipping magnate Aristotélis Onássis and the operatic diva Maria Callas have all stayed here. Why not dig out your phone and relive the amazing voice of this opera singer while wandering past? *C3–4*

SOKRÁKI

11km (6.8 miles) / 30-min drive from Dafníla

Driving to Sokráki is quite an experience if you take the road from Áno Korakiána. The tarmac road is mostly only single-lane, and winds like a corkscrew up a steep slope with 23 hair-pin bends (and even more gentle ones) revealing breathtaking views of central and southern Corfu. Luckily, there are several passing places where you can stop and take pictures of the road and the spectacular views. Passengers usually have sweaty hands when they finally reach Sokráki, and the driver will need to have a sit down after all their hard work. The best place to do that is on the tiny village square, where two unspoilt *kafenía* serve refreshing drinks and snacks. *C3*

PÉLEKAS, GLIFÁDA & MIRTIÓTISSA

(C5) **The large mountain village of Pélekas (pop. 565) has lost its flair over the years. Just ten years ago, hundreds of metres of walls here were covered in artistic graffiti and a large international street festival was held every year. Those days are gone, and the village now only attracts those in search of nostalgia and romance.**

The village's scene has gradually relocated to *Glifáda Beach* in summer, a 2-km / 1.2-mile stretch of sand. In the days where there were no hotels along the seafront, backpackers were shuttled down to the seaside by bus. Today, the beach is firmly in the grip of mass tourism and the newly built hotel complexes try to keep guests on their sites. Despite this, Pélekas is still worth a visit, if only to watch the sun set behind the hillside rather than into the sea.

SIGHTSEEING

KAISER'S THRONE ★
During his stays on Corfu, the German Kaiser Wilhelm II was fond of a small rock on the top of the hill (*Sunset Point*) that towers above Pélekas where he would sit and and watch the

VERSATILE LITTLE ORANGES

Corfu's most famous speciality is the ⚑ kumquat *(koum kouát)*. Corfu is the only place in Europe where they are grown as a cash crop. The fruit – which is the size of a small plum and originally came from China – was first brought to the island by the British in the first half of the 19th century. Like oranges, they ripen in winter and can be picked between January and March. Corfiot companies use them to make various liqueurs: a colourless one from the flesh of the fruit and one that is bright pink from the skins. Kumquats are often made into jam, sold candied and can be eaten fresh during the harvest. The skin can be eaten as well; it gives the fruit its tangy aroma. If you want to see how these fruits grow on Corfu, you can best do so by driving to Nímfes in the north of the island where particularly many of these trees thrive.

sunset. Today, you can drive up here from the village following the signs along the tarmac road and toast the sunset with a cocktail from the hotel bar. This natural spectacle is particularly special in June, when it is magnificent. At that time of year, it looks like a red ball of fire is rolling down the Corfiot hills, with the sun seeming to first settle on a mountaintop before continuing on its journey downwards at the same angle as the slope.

INSIDER TIP
A sunset worth filming

PANAGÍA MIRTIÓTISSA (MONÍ MYRTIDIÓN) MONASTERY

Just 200m / 650ft from the nudist beaches of Mirtiótissa, one of the most beautifully located monasteries on the island lies hidden between olive trees, banana plants and countless flowers. According to legend, a Turk who had converted to Christianity founded it in the 14th century after he had discovered an icon of Maria in a myrtle bush. However, the present buildings date from the 19th century. Today, just one monk lives in the monastery; he keeps it in order and would like to revitalise the old oil mill. *Daily 9am–1pm and 5–9pm | it is easy to miss the signpost so keep a good eye out between Pélekas and the Rópa Valley; access is via a narrow road, which is tarmacked at first and then cemented | car park (chargeable) half way up; limited parking on the beach and near the monastery*

Panagía Mirtiótissa Monastery: just one solitary monk inhabits this heavenly spot

EATING & DRINKING

ROÚLA 🍴
Eat well on a budget. This family-run taverna is situated just off the village square and is one of the best-value eateries in central Corfu. The proprietor, Roúla, is always in a good mood, and loves serving her family's own wine in the restaurant. *Daily | on Pélekas' main street | €*

SPORT & ACTIVITIES

The beaches at both Pélekas and Glifáda have a good range of options for those wanting to try some water sports out.

BEACHES

The secluded, approximately 300-m / 984-ft-long, sandy beach at ★🏄 *Mirtiótissa* is unofficially used as a nudist beach. So far, only a limited number of sun beds and umbrellas have been available for hire, but there is a certain amount of shade among the rocks. This beach is really something and well worth visiting, no matter where you are staying on Corfu.

🏄 *Glifáda Beach*, on the other hand, is usually very crowded but there are plenty of sun beds, umbrellas and water-sports activities. Two narrow tarmac roads lead down to 🏄 *Pélekas Beach* (also known as *Kontogialós Beach*), which is 500m / 1,640ft long, not quite as busy and also suitable for children. At its southern tip, it merges into the much smaller, but no less beautiful, 🏄 *Yaliskári Beach*.

The only way to reach all four beaches from Pélekas is down the steep road on foot or by car; an off-road vehicle is required for the route down to Mirtiótissa beach. Despite this, the beach is often extremely busy.

WELLNESS

The *Aegeo Spa* in the Hotel Mayor Pélekas Monastery *(tel. 26 61 18 06 00 | mayorpelekasmonastery.com)* is the biggest spa in the area. Non-hotel guests are required to book ahead.

NIGHTLIFE

The nightlife is concentrated in the cafés and bars around the village square and surrounding alleyways.

PÉLEKAS CAFÉ
This modern café on the small main square is a meeting place for both locals and holiday-makers in the evening. The village priest even drops by regularly. There is Greek and international music, and you have a good view of the island through the wide, open windows. The visitors' book is always open too, and is full of praise for the friendly atmosphere. *Daily | Pélekas*

ZANSI BAR
This tiny music bar has not changed since it opened in 1980: crowds of guests gather inside and outside to drink and chat all year round. The dancing starts when rock 'n' roll is played (if not before). *Daily from 9pm at the earliest | village square*

When the sun goes down you'll find space and tranquility on the beach at Érmones

AROUND PÉLEKAS, GLIFÁDA & MIRTIÓTISSA

4 RÓPA VALLEY

6km (3.7 miles) / 10-min drive from Pélekas

Ever wondered what attracts so many people to the game of golf? Then spend a few hours watching the players at Corfu Golf Club from its restaurant veranda (open to the public) and you may learn why. It is, however, hardly a Greek experience – you will feel as if you are in an English landscaped park. The small modern chapel next to it is the only hint that you are not in fact in the Home Counties. *C4–5*

5 ÉRMONES

7km (4.3 miles) / 15-min drive from Pélekas

Today, as in ancient times, Homer's Odysseus would certainly rub his eyes in disbelief on awakening from a deep sleep on the beach at Érmones after his ten year journey home. Maybe he would see a bathing beauty as lovely as Nausicaa, the daughter of King Alcinous of Phaeacia, standing in front of him. However, he would certainly not recognise the surroundings. The hinterland is now covered with a sprawl of hotels and guesthouses. Odysseus would be equally surprised to see the funicular that ferries guests staying at the *Grand Mediterraneo Resort Hotel* from their rooms high up on the slope down to the beach, which – at just 200m / 656ft long – is not really one of Corfu's most beautiful. However, the sports possibilities near the hotels are good and varied. *C5*

6 SINARÁDES

6km (3.7 miles) / 10-min drive from Pélekas

Do you know what a birthing chair is? With two of them in its collection, the ★ *Folklore Museum (Mon–Sat 9am–2pm | admission 2 euros | signposted at the church; leave your vehicle at the car park in the village centre) in Sinarádes* (pop. 1,120) gives you a chance to find out. The exhibition on the two floors of this historical building, which was occupied as a house until 1970, shows what rural life was like for Corfiots between 1860 and 1960. There are excellent descriptions of all the exhibits in English. Alongside the birthing chairs, figurines for the Greek shadow play *karagióssi* are among the highlights of the exhibition.

It is worth taking a short stroll through the village with its many old houses after you have visited the museum. Those that are almost completely overgrown with flowers are particularly lovely. If you want to soak up the down-to-earth, local atmosphere, have a drink in one of the old-fashioned grocery stores-cum-*kafenía* on the road and watch village life go by.

INSIDER TIP
Have a drink with the locals

One of these is *Sinarádes (€)* right on the *platía*. Stelíos, the owner, organises a barbeque for his guests in the evening. In the high season, a lamb is roasted on a spit on Sundays. ⊞ C6

BETTER PLACES TO STAY

STONE COTTAGES

At *Casa Lucia*, guests stay in lovingly and tastefully restored stone cottages from Corfu's Venetian period. The pool is embedded in a tropical garden full of blossoming flowers. A taverna serving vegan food is situated just 300m / 990ft from the cottages and the next beach is 3km / 1.8 miles away. You can also take part in yoga, tai-chi and qigong courses. *10 rooms | Sgombroú | 150m / 492ft to the left of the national road from Dassiá to Paleokastrítsa | tel. 26 61 09 14 19 |casa-lucia-corfu.com | €€ | ⊞ C4*

SLEEP IN A PRESIDENTIAL SUITE

If you after a unique place to stay on Corfu, the *Pélekas Country Club*, once a Venetian stately home, is hard to beat. Stables and other courtyard buildings have been transformed into spacious, ground-floor apartments decorated with antique furniture. Living up to its name, the presidential suite in the main building once accommodated the French President François Mitterrand and the Greek Prime Minister Geórgios Papandréou. The club's pool and bar are located in luxurious parkland. The hotel also has its own helipad. *10 rooms | km 8 on the road from Kérkyra to Pélekas | tel. 26 61 05 29 18 | country-club.gr | €€€ | ⊞ C5*

DISCOVERY TOURS

Want to get under the skin of the region? Then our discovery tours are just the thing for you – they include terrific tips for stops worth making, breathtaking places to visit, selected restaurants and fun activities.

❶ CORFU AT A GLANCE

➤ The whole of Corfu at your feet
➤ Swim in the Canal d'Amour
➤ Find out if Roger Moore discovered Corfu's best coffee

📍 Kérkyra (Corfu Town)   🏁 Kérkyra (Corfu Town)

🔄 225km / 140 miles   🚗 2 days
                              (4.5 hrs total driving time)

ℹ️ This tour will first take you up to the island's north before heading south for the second day. If you are staying in the island's central region, you can easily do this tour from your accommodation without relocating.

Kaiser's Throne

CLIMB THE HIGHEST MOUNTAIN AND SPEND TIME ON CORFU'S MOST BEAUTIFUL CAPE

The tour starts in ❶ Kérkyra ➤ p. 38 *and then contin-ues on past the holiday resorts of Kontokáli, Gouviá and Dassiá to Pírgi. From Pírgi, take the coastal road and turn up a narrow, twisting road with hairpin bends to Spartilás. Shortly before reaching Sgourádes, head right* up to the tranquil mountain village of ❷ Strinílas ➤ p. 72, where you can take a break at the village square under the shade of its ancient elm tree. Now head up to ❸ Pantokrátor ➤ p. 72, the island's high-est point at 906m / 2,972ft high. The panoramic view over the island and far into the Albanian and Northern Greek mountains is breathtaking. After attempting to turn your vehicle round on the narrow mountain ridge (which could prove to be a rather hair-raising experi-ence!), *drive down to the northern coast and take a left onto the road that goes round the island*. You will pass the holiday resorts of Acharávi and Róda, and at Sidári ➤ p. 71 treat yourself to a dip in the ❹ Canal d'Amour ➤ p. 71 before *continuing in the direction of Perouládes*. But first a quick *detour to* ❺ Cape Drástis ➤ p. 71, and then stop for lunch in one of the two tavernas at the steep harbour in ❻ Perouládes ➤ p. 70. The route

DAY 1	
❶ Kérkyra	
30km	25 mins
❷ Strinílas	
5km	5 mins
❸ Pantokrátor	
27km	25 Mins
❹ Canal d'Amour	
5km	5 mins
❺ Cape Drástis	
1km	2 mins
❻ Perouládes	

❼ Afiónas

7km   6 mins

then *passes Avliótes to the beach of Ágios Stéfanos and further up through Arillás to* ❼ Afiónas ➤ p. 75. Drive up to the village's church where this road will then end.

On the square itself, you can buy excellent-quality Corfiot olive oil; the owners, Heidi and Rainer Kalkmann, also make sensational olive pastes and dips. Follow the alley on the left of the olive

INSIDER TIP
Get a taste of Corfu

oil shop for a few metres until you reach *Taverne Ánemos*, which offers excellent views of the bays of Aríllas and Ágios Geórgios.

LICENCE TO FIL(-TER COFFEE)

Then *cross Ágios Geórgios North* ➤ p. 75 via ❽ Pági with its Spiros Bond 008 Cafe, where Roger Moore spent his time between takes of the 1979 James Bond film *For Your Eyes Only*. Then *carry on to Makrádes* and the castle ❾ Angelókastro ➤ p. 81. After a 10-minute steep uphill march on foot, you will reach the top with a splendid view along the wild, steep coastline. Then enjoy an afternoon coffee on one of the restaurants' terraces in ❿ Lákones ➤ p. 80, which resemble balconies in the sky, and from which there is a wonderful view down to the olive trees and cypresses on Paleokastrítsa ➤ p. 77. For many Corfiots, this is the most beautiful place on earth. It will now be too late to visit the monastery, so plan to return another day to explore it at leisure (can be reached by bus). *Turn left immediately on entering Paleokastrítsa and then take a right straight afterwards* towards the large mountain village of ⓫ Pélekas ➤ p. 107, through the lush green Rópa

❽ Pági	
7km	6 mins

❾ Angelókastro	
4km	4 mins

❿ Lákones	
20km	20 mins

⓫ Pélekas	

There's always a reason to celebrate – including in the pretty mountain village of Afiónas

Valley. You will probably reach the village in time to watch the sunset from the Kaiser's Throne ➤ p. 107. In the evening, you can either eat up here or head down to one of the tavernas in the village of Pélekas. The village also offers basic and affordable accommodation if you do not want to return to your hotel for the night.

DAY 2

⑫ Sinarádes
4km 4 mins

⑬ Ágios Górdis
4km 4 mins

⑭ Pendáti
8km 8 mins

⑮ Paramónas
6km 6 mins

⑯ Gardíki
3km 3 mins

⑰ Lake Koríssion
16km 15 mins

⑱ Ágios Geórgios South
13km 13 mins

⑲ Lefkími
19km 20 mins

PANORAMIC COASTAL VIEWS

Start the next day by *driving from Pélekas* to ⑫ Sinarádes ➤ p. 111 along a very picturesque road which takes you through the village and to the snack bar Locanda on the village square. It is worth visiting the village's folklore museum. On the *drive down to* ⑬ Ágios Górdis ➤ p. 86 take in one of the island's most beautiful coastal landscapes. *Shortly after Ágios Górdis, a narrow tarmac road branches off at a right angle to the village of* ⑭ Pendáti ➤ p. 87 where you can enjoy your second coffee break of the morning accompanied by a panoramic view on the Chris Place terrace. *The narrow, bendy road continues* on close to the coast and through an enchanting forest full of century-old olive trees to ⑮ Paramónas ➤ p. 88 an excellent spot for a swim. Follow the road through the enchanted forest to the important fortification of ⑯ Gardíki ➤ p. 94, which dates back to the 13th century.

DUNES FOR AS FAR AS THE EYE CAN SEE

The route then turns *to the coast* through vineyards and meadows of cut flowers to ⑰ Lake Koríssion ➤ p. 92 with long, thin stretches of dunes in front of it. Alonáki taverna, located at the northern end of the lake in Chalikúnas, is a good place to eat lunch in this green paradise. *Now drive past the castle of Gardíki again and inland around Lake Koríssion* to the resort of ⑱ Ágios Geórgios South ➤ p. 92, which stretches along the sea for almost 3km / 1.9 miles against a backdrop of stunning dunes. The main road brings you to the small town of ⑲ Lefkími ➤ p. 94, where you should definitely plan a small detour to the picturesque river port. On your way back north, *exit the island's main road near Perivóli and head to the coast by taking the road in*

Perivóli to Kalivótis. Your route now takes you *back north directly along the sea.* It is worth taking a coffee break at Nótos Beach in the Panórama taverna garden near ⑳ Petríti ➤ p. 91. At the fishing port in Petríti, the *narrow coastal road takes you past Boúkari,* with its many good fish tavernas, to the two connected villages of ㉑ Messongí and Moraítika ➤ p. 88 where you can also eat well. It takes just 30 minutes by car back *to the island's capital* ❶ Kérkyra where your tour will end.

⑳ Petríti	
8km	8 mins

㉑ Messongí-Moraítika	
20km	20 mins

| ❶ Kérkyra | |

❷ ANCIENT KÉRKYRA – A WALKING TOUR OUTSIDE THE OLD TOWN

➤ A rural walk around the city
➤ See where Prince Philip was born
➤ Have a picnic in an ancient temple

📍 Football stadium in Kérkyra

🏁 Anemómilos windmill

🔄 6km / 3.7 miles

🚶 3-4 hours / (1.5 hrs total walking time)

ℹ️ City bus 15 takes you to the stadium, city bus 2a from Anemómilos takes you back to the city centre. There is a bus stop at the park entrance of Mon Repos.

START THE DAY AMONG RUINS

The walk starts at the ❶ football Stadium in Kérkyra in close proximity to the airport. *Starting out from the eastern side of the stadium, the route takes you first of all to the city's main cemetery* with its ❷ cemetery church, which contains three valuable icons. *A very narrow tarmac lane leads you out of the cemetery* and after 80m / 262ft, you will see the only remains of the ancient ❸ city wall of Kérkyra; 17 stone layers from the 15th century have remained just as they were placed in the new construction of a basilica in early Christian times.

❶ Football stadium in Kérkyra

| ❷ Cemetery church |

| ❸ City wall of Kérkyra |

One of the highlights of this tour is the small classical castle of Mon Repos

④ Artemis Temple

⑤ Ágii Theodóri

Follow the lane further past some plain farmhouses; sheep graze, chickens peck and dogs laze about in the sunshine. A few minutes later you will come across the scanty remains of the ancient ④ Artemis Temple, in whose excavation Germany's Emperor Wilhelm II took great interest. It is right in front of the walls of the ⑤ Ágii Theodóri convent; one of the nuns who lives there will be pleased to show you around the convent church.

ONWARDS TO A PALACE AND ITS GARDEN

Stay on the small lane and *turn right onto the main road*, go past a research institute for olive cultivation and a primary school in traditional classical architecture. A short distance further and you will be at the grand entrance to the Mon Repos palace park (you can't miss it). Here you can admire the view of the romantic, old walls from the wonderful green area surrounding the ❻ Palaiópolis Basilica ➤ p. 48 and see the excavations underneath a modern tent roof where ❼ Roman baths have been excavated. Now enter ❽ Mon Repos' grounds ➤ p. 48. Start off by visiting the small palace of ❾ Mon Repos, where Philip, the late husband of Queen Elizabeth II, was born on 10 June, 1921 as a Greek Prince. Then follow the signs to the *Doric Temple. At the first junction, take a left along the shady path through the woods down to a small* ❿ bathing bay completely enclosed by trees with a jetty where you can take a quick dip. This is probably where Empress Sisi and members of the German Imperial family went swimming.

❻	**Palaiópolis Basilica**
❼	**Roman baths**
❽	**Mon Repos' grounds**
❾	**Mon Repos**
❿	**Bathing bay**

The *main path* will take you past what is left of the Temple of Hera to the extremely romantic foundations of the Doric ⓫ Temple of Kardáki which dates back to the fifth century BCE. Some of its columns have been re-erected amid the greenery and make a good photo opportunity. Very few visitors come here and there is no attendant, so feel free to unpack your picnic and tuck in surrounded by the temple's ancient columns. *A very narrow, in parts overgrown, path starting at the south-east corner of the temple area takes you to* the low wall surrounding the castle park. If you climb over it and *keep right on the path alongside the wall you will reach the tiny hamlet of Análipsi. Here, you can follow the tarmac path along the castle wall back to the entrance and then follow the main road to the right.*

INSIDER TIP
Picnic in a temple

TO CAP IT ALL: A COOL, REFRESHING DIP

You will pass the entrance to the ⑫ Agías Efthímias convent ➤ p. 48 with its splendid courtyard. Shortly afterwards, you will reach the ⑬ Mon Repos Lido ➤ p. 55 – the only beach in this part of the city – and the ⑭ Anemómilos windmill with the Café Nautilus, where you can end your afternoon with a splendid view of the Old Fort and the old town of Corfu.

⑫ Agías Efthímias convent

⑬ Mon Repos Lido

⑭ Anemómilos windmil

❸ VILLAGES AND BEACHES AROUND PANTOKRÁTOR

➤ Test your nerves on the "corkscrew road"
➤ Take a walk around a ghost town
➤ Discover Corfu's most beautiful coastal village

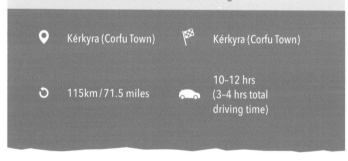

📍 Kérkyra (Corfu Town)   🏁 Kérkyra (Corfu Town)

↻ 115km / 71.5 miles   🚗 10-12 hrs (3-4 hrs total driving time)

SHARPEN YOUR NERVES ON HAIRPIN BENDS

From the town of ❶ Kérkyra ➤ p. 38 take the national road *in the direction of Paleokastrítsa before following the signs to the large mountain village of* Áno Korakiána ➤ p. 105 with its beautiful old houses. Then *follow the signs to Sokráki and Zigós.* The road now becomes narrower and winds like a corkscrew up the steep slope. When you arrive in ❷ Sokráki ➤ p. 106 with its narrow road through the town, you might need to stop for a coffee or a glass of the typical Corfiot lemonade *tzizimbírra.* Then *drive downhill slightly* before starting your ascent of Pantokrátor. Let yourself be tempted to take a break in the village of ❸ Strinílas ➤ p. 72 at the Taverna Oasis and sit under a more than

❶ Kérkyra
25km   25 mins

❷ Sokráki
10km   10 mins

❸ Strinílas
5km   5 mins

200-year-old elm tree on the village square. The entire island of Corfu lies spread out beneath you when you reach the summit of ❹ **Pantokrátor** ➤ p. 72.

FROLIC IN THE WATER AND THEN VISIT A GHOST TOWN

Back on the main road, return to Petalia and then *head north to the coast* until you reach *Acharávi* ➤ p. 66 and there take a right to bring you to your next destination: ❺ **Ágios Spirídonas** ➤ p. 69, where you can choose to go for a swim and have something to eat. But you might prefer to have lunch in the next village on the

❹ Pantokrátor	
21km	20 mins

❺ Ágios Spirídonas	
10km	20 mins

Mítsos Taverna is a wonderful place to finish your tour around Pantokrátor

6 Paleó Períthia
13km 15 mins

7 Kassiópi
20km 20 mins

tour: the old Venetian settlement of **6 Paleó Períthia** ➤ p. 73. After a stroll through the ghost village of Paleó Períthia, *carry on back to the coast to* **7 Kassiópi** ➤ p. 62. The best way to soak in the beauty of this place is to take the 25-minute walk around the peninsula with its castle. On the way you will pass Batería Beach, which is a splendid spot for bathing and snorkelling and also has a good taverna.

Drive back *to the south along the coastal road*. Ágios Stéfanos Siniés ➤ p. 65, close to Albania, Kouloúra ➤ p. 66 with its circular harbour and Kalámi ➤ p. 66 are all well worth a look and offer good photo opportunities. However, you should definitely drive down to

8 Nissáki
23km 25 mins

the old port in **8 Nissáki** and let the day come to a close on the terrace of the Mítsos taverna near the sea or go to the tiny beach for a last dip. The road round the island then becomes less bendy and *you'll be back in*

1 Kérkyra

1 Kérkyra *in about half an hour.*

④ SHOPPING CORFU STYLE – BETWEEN GOUVIÁ AND PALEOKASTRÍTSA

➤ Fresh local delicacies from a famous baker
➤ Visit a leather workshop
➤ Explore the deep blue sea while keeping your feet dry

📍 Gouviá, at the traffic light crossroads

🏁 Paleokastrítsa

→ 15km / 9.3 miles

🚗 2–6 hrs (30 mins total driving time)

ℹ️ Important: credit cards are rarely accepted

THE HUNT FOR THE BEST SOUVENIRS

Soon after *turning off the road round the island at* ① Gouviá ➤ p. 100 you can stock up with delicious baked Corfiot pastries at the popular ② Emeral Bakery on the left. There is an enormous selection of freshly baked goods and extremely affordable coffee here. Then continue and *on the right-hand* side you will see Sofoklís Ikonomídis and Sissy Moskídu's ③ ceramic

① Gouviá	
1.5km	2 mins
② Emeral Bakery	
2km	2 mins
③ Ceramic workshop	

workshop where they create, fire and paint colourful ceramic objects on the premises. After another few minutes in the car, visit the ④ olive-wood carving exhibition *on the left of the road*. Shortly afterwards, you will reach the ⑤ Mavromátis distillery *on the right*, where the company's liqueurs can be purchased in the modern, air-conditioned showroom. *600m/2,000ft further on, a no-through-road off to the left to the Hotel*

④ Olive-wood carving

1km   1 mins

⑤ Mavromátis

800m   1 mins

As a break from shopping, admire the mosaics at Paleokastrítsa monastery

Fundána will lead you past a traditionally painted country house. This is where ⑥ Níkos Sakális produces and sells high-quality leather bags, glasses cases, backpacks and book covers (follow signs to the "Leather Workshop"). All of his products bear the "Seminole" trademark. The visit to the leather workshop ends the shopping tour. Perhaps now you're ready for a relaxing swim, or just wish to enjoy the countryside or a bit of culture. You can have all of these things, *after a ten-minute drive to the coast,* at ⑦ Paleokastrítsa ➤ p. 77. First visit the monastery, then the Corfu Aquarium. Follow with a trip on a glass-bottomed boat, before completing your trip with a dip at the beach that sits on the narrow stretch between the village and the monastery.

⑥ Níkos Sakális	
6km	6 mins

⑦ Paleokastrítsa	
6km	6 mins

⑤ BOAT TRIP TO ALBANIA

➤ Explore a country barely anyone goes to
➤ See an ancient site far better preserved than anything on Corfu
➤ Enjoy delicious fresh fish on the harbour quay

📍 Kérkyra ferry harbour

🏁 Kérkyra ferry harbour

⇄ Ferry 30km / 18 miles, Taxi 40km / 25 miles

🚢 1 day (30–75-min ferry trip, plus 50 mins in a taxi in Albania)

ℹ Don't forget your passport! Albania is one hour ahead of Corfu all year round. Ferry timetables available at *www.ionian-cruises.com.*

A FERRY (AND A TAXI) AWAY FROM THE ANCIENT CITY OF BUTRINT

Depending on which ferry you take, the crossing from ① Kérkyra ferry harbour takes 30–75 minutes *to the port in Albania, located at the small coastal town of* ② Saranda, which the Greeks call Ágíi Saránda. Although it only has 35,000 inhabitants, the many new

① Kérkyra ferry harbour	
30km	30–75 mins
② Saranda	

and large buildings give it the appearance of being much larger. However, many of the apartments sit empty for most of the year; Albanians working abroad have bought them as an investment and are seldom here. Immediately after the passport control at the ferry harbour, taxis are waiting that you can hire for approximately two hours to take you to the excavations at Butrint. *The road takes you across the narrow strip of land between the sea and Lake Butrint* known as the ❸ Vivari Channel. The entrance to the excavation site of ancient ❹ Butrint *(daily 9am–6pm)* is extremely close to the channel. The mountains you can see across the water are on mainland Greece.

❸ Vivari Channel
❹ Butrint
6km   6 mins

The city of Butrint was founded around 1200 BCE and was inhabited for more than 2,800 years. It experienced its golden age in the Roman period, and most of its –

often well-preserved – historical monuments date back to this period. Today, ancient Butrint is listed as a UNESCO World Heritage Site. The archaeological site lies on a peninsula jutting into Lake Butrint that rises up to a height of 30m / 100ft. It is densely wooded but the 50-minute walk seems like a stroll through a park. Information boards in English with diagrams and artists' reconstructions provide a thorough explanation of what can be seen at the site: Roman baths and a Roman theatre, the baptistery of an early-Christian basilica that has been preserved up as far as roof level, the partially very well preserved city walls, and several city gates from various periods. After visiting the excavation site, you can enjoy a coffee in the pretty garden of the Hotel Butrint. *On your return to Saranda*, your taxi driver will be happy to show you the pretty beaches of ❺ Ksamil with a view of the off-shore islets.

Remnants of Albania's grand past: ancient Butrint

ENJOY THE HARBOUR TOWN OF SARANDA

In ⑥ Saranda *let the taxi driver drop you off at the marina where you can enjoy an affordable meal in an attractive setting at the* Limani *restaurant.* Then *turn left at the Hotel Porto Eda and head into the city, taking another left at the first crossroads.* You will soon reach the town's main square with its small green area and the remnants of the early Christian Agía Saránda basilica dating back to the sixth century, which is set behind fences. It's now just a ten-minute walk back to the ferry harbour from where ferries and hydrofoils head back to ① Kérkyra ferry harbour.

⑥ Saranda	
30km	30 mins

① Kérkyra ferry harbour

GOOD TO KNOW
HOLIDAY BASICS

ARRIVAL

+ 2 hours time difference

Greece is two hours ahead of Greenwich Mean Time, seven hours ahead of US Eastern Time and seven hours behind Australian Eastern Time.

GETTING THERE

Many airlines fly to Corfu in summer and there are flights via Athens throughout the year. The flight from London takes around 3¼ hours. Corfu's airport is on the outskirts of the town. You can easily take a taxi to your hotel – the fare to the centre of town should cost 10–15 euros. In addition, the number 15 bus connects the airport to the coach terminal in Kérkyra and to Platia Sarocco in the city centre – from where you can change to buses to any corner of the town. It departs at least once an hour and tickets cost 1.20 euro.

In the summer months, there are several daily connections with the Italian ports of Ancona, Bari, Brindisi and Venice. Depending on the ship, the crossing from Brindisi takes 3½–8 hours; from Ancona, around 20 hours; and 29–36 hours from Venice. Compare prices at *gtp.gr, greekferries. gr, minoan.gr, superfast.com* or contact a travel agent.

GETTING IN

You can travel to Greece without a visa so long as your stay does not exceed 90 days. If you intend to stay for longer, check which visa you require with the Greek embassy. On arrival, your passport must have at least three months

The coast off Paleokastrítsa

validity after your point of departure from Greece.

CLIMATE & WHEN TO GO

The high season on Corfu lasts from May to mid-October. Many hotels and most restaurants outside of the island's capital are closed in the other months. In May, the sea can still be too cold for swimming, but this is the month when the flowers are at their best. The water is pleasantly warm in autumn, but by this time the vegetation is largely withered and burnt. It hardly rains between June and September, but there are often very strong winds.

The capital, Kérkyra, is also an attractive winter destination. There are almost no holidaymakers during this period and the locals have time to enjoy themselves in the tavernas. There will be fires blazing in the open hearths in the bars, restaurants and cafés – and you will have the museums all to yourself!

Electricity

You will need a UK–EU adapter for your devices.

GETTING AROUND

BUS

Buses are the mode of public transport on Corfu. You must purchase tickets in advance from kiosks, ticket machines or in your hotel. Bus number 2 takes you to the ferry port, Mon Repos and Kanóni; number 7 to Dassiá; number 5 to Kinopiástes;

number 6 to Benítses; number 8 to Ágios Ioánnis; number 10 to Achíllio; number 11 to Pélekas. Line 15 connects the airport to the coach terminal, city centre and new ferry port. Bus number 16 connects the old port to the cruise ship terminal if cruise ships are docked in the port. If possible, you should buy your tickets for long-distance buses/coaches at the bus station – otherwise, when you get on the bus. Timetables for city buses can be found at *astikoktelkerkyras.gr*, for coaches at *greenbuses.gr*.

VEHICLE HIRE

Bicycles, mopeds, motor scooters, motorbikes, 4x4s and cars can be rented in all of the holiday resorts on Corfu. Hiring a Vauxhall Corsa begins at around 35 euros per day. If you want to hire a car or motorbike, you have to be at least 23 years of age. Be

careful: even if you have full insurance cover, damage to the tyres and the underside of the car is not covered. No matter how small the accident, you should call the police – otherwise, the insurance company will not pay. And, if you rent a moped, it is a good idea to wear jeans even if the weather is hot; they will provide increased protection if you have an accident and fall off.

There is a good network of petrol stations on the island and all sell both petrol and diesel. Most garages are open daily from 8am to 8pm. Self-service is still uncommon and coin-operated petrol stations are rare. Fuel prices are considerably higher than in many other countries in Europe.

The speed limit is 50kph and 90kph on main roads. It is compulsory to wear seatbelts in the front seats. The blood alcohol limit is 0.5; 0.2 for motorbike riders. The fines for traffic offences are extremely high. The police usually demand 60 euros for illegal parking, which must be paid to the authority stated on the ticket.

TAXI

There are plenty of taxis in Kérkyra. You can flag them down, get in at the taxi ranks or telephone for one. The prices are set by the government and are comparatively low (e.g. airport–town centre 10–15 euros). But, make sure that the taxi driver uses tariff 1 within the city limits; tariff 2 only applies to cross-country trips!

FESTIVALS & EVENTS
ALL YEAR ROUND

JANUARY

Blessing of the Waters and Baptism of Christ On the morning of 6 January, in coastal villages/towns, believers jump into the sea to retrieve a cross which a priest has thrown in.

FEBRUARY/MARCH

Carnival processions In Kérkyra on the last three Sundays and the ⚑ Wednesday before Shrove Monday. On Shrove Monday in Messongí.

MARCH/APRIL

Good Friday Lots of processions in the capital, starting in the afternoon (photo).

Holy Saturday Corfiots throw hundreds of clay jugs filled with water from balconies onto the main streets in the Old Town. At 11pm, mass is held, followed by fireworks.

Easter Sunday Grilled lamb is prepared on a spit in every village.

JUNE

Folk dances Performed at Kérkyra's theatre by local school children to mark the end of the school year.

Firewalking On 24 June in Bénitses, in an ancient tradition, brave locals walk and dance on red hot coals.

JULY/AUGUST

Festival Kerkyras Around 15 concerts are held in Kérkyra and Glifáda Beach across a broad range of genres including theatre music. *festivalkerkyras.gr*

Feast of the Virgin Mary On 14/15 August in Kassiópi and Paleokastrítsa, folkloric traditions accompany the religious festival.

SEPTEMBER

Wine Festival In Arillás where music, dance and a BBQ accompany the wine-making process. *arillas.com*

International Choir Festival and Competition In Kérkyra, at the theatre and Old Fort, 40 choirs from 20 countries perform. *interkultur.com/de/events*

Corfu Beer Festival In Arillás, music, dance and a local-produce market takes over the town. *corfubeer-festival.com*

EMERGENCIES

CONSULATES & EMBASSIES
British Vice consulate
18 Mantzarou Street 491 00, Kérkyra | tel. 26 61 03 00 55 / 26 61 02 34 57 | gov. uk/world/organisations/british-vice-consulate-corfu | Email: Corfu@fco.gov.uk

U.S. Embassy (ATHENS)
91 Vasilisis Sophias Avenue | 10160 Athens | tel. 21 07 21 29 51 | gr.usembassy.gov/embassy-consulate/Athens

EMERGENCY SERVICES
112 – for the police, fire brigade and ambulance
171 – for the tourist police

HEALTH
Well-trained doctors guarantee basic medical care. However, there is often a lack of medical equipment. The standard of the government hospital in Kérkyra is low. Complicated cases are sent to Athens.

If you are seriously ill or injured, you should try to fly home. Emergency treatment in hospitals and government health centres (ESY, National Health Centre) is free of charge. It is highly recommended that you take out international health insurance; you can then choose your doctor, pay him in cash, get a receipt and then present your bills to the insurance company for refunding.

Chemists are well-stocked but do not always have British medication. In Greece, many medicines that are only available if you have a prescription in other countries can be purchased without one and are cheaper than at home – e.g. painkillers and remedies for heartburn and herpes. You are only able to import small quantities.

Mosquitoes also like Corfu. You should have mosquito protection in your first-aid kit as well as something for insect bites. Bathing shoes will protect you from sea urchins. There are no poisonous snakes or scorpions on the island.

GREEK ALPHABET

A	α	a	N	ν	n
B	β	v, w	Ξ	ξ	ks, x
Γ	γ	g, i	O	o	o
Δ	δ	d	Π	π	p
E	ε	e	P	ρ	r
Z	ζ	s, z	Σ	σ, ς	s, ss
H	η	i	T	τ	t
Θ	θ	th	Y	υ	i, y
Ι	ι	i, j	Φ	φ	f
K	κ	k	X	χ	ch
Λ	λ	l	Ψ	ψ	ps
M	μ	m	Ω	ω	o

ESSENTIALS

ACCOMMODATION
There are plenty of places to stay on Corfu. You will find the widest range of options on the coast, but some inland villages, like Pélekas, Ágios Ioánnis and Paléo Períthia, also have plenty of hotels, guesthouses and apartments. *Booking.com* will give you as good a sense of what is available as anything. It is, however, often worth booking directly with the accommodation.

There are a large number of apartments on the island alongside its numerous hotels. Finding a detached villa or holiday home can be trickier.

There are no youth hostels on the island, so budget travellers are best advised to seek out one of the many campsites.

CUSTOMS

EU citizens can import and export the following goods for their personal use tax-free: 800 cigarettes, 1kg tobacco, 90 litres of wine, 10 litres of spirits over 22%, 110 litres of beer.

Non-EU citizens can import and export the following goods for their personal use tax-free: 200 cigarettes, 250g tobacco, 4 litres of wine, 1 litre of spirits over 22%, 16 litres of beer. https://greece.visahq.com/customs/

ENTRANCE FEES

A joint ticket for the Archaeological Museum, Museum of Asian Art, the Byzantine Museum and Old Fortress is available at the ticket desk of any one of the four institutions for 14 euros. This represents a saving of 6 euros compared to the price of separate tickets.

National museums give discounts to pensioners over 65 years of age. Children from EU countries and students with an International Student Card are granted free admission.

There is free entry to most museums on 6 March and the last weekend in September, and for a range of festivals, including the International Day for Monuments and Sites in April, International Museum Day in May, International Environment Day in June, and World Tourism Day in September. Out of the main tourism season, most museums are free on the first Sunday of each month.

There is no entrance fee for visiting churches and monasteries, but donations are always welcome. The most discreet way to do this is to buy candles and light them in front of an icon with an optional prayer of intercession.

HOW MUCH DOES IT COST?

Bus	0.21 euro
	per kilometre
Coffee	2.50 euro
	for a cup of coffee
Pedal boat	10 euro
	per hour
Wine	3.50 euro
	for a glass of wine
Snack	2.50 euro
	for gýros
Petrol	1.70 euro
	per litre premium

INTERNET & WIFI

Freshly laid strips of tarmac are visible along the roads in many Corfu villages. The reason is that fibre-optic cables have been installed all over Corfu. In keeping with the Greeks' understanding of democracy, free Wifi is available

INSIDER TIP
Free Wifi for everyone

almost everywhere on Corfu, in *tavernas*, bars and simple *kafenía* – except in some luxury hotels. The password is usually the phone number or the sequence of digits 1 to 9 followed by a 0.

LANGUAGE

The Greeks are proud of their unique alphabet. Although place names and labels are often also written in Roman letters, it is still useful to have some knowledge of the Greek alphabet – and you need to know how to stress the words correctly to be understood; the vowel with the accent is emphasised.

MONEY & CREDIT CARDS

The national currency is the euro. You can withdraw money from many ATMs with your credit or debit card. Banks and post offices cash traveller's cheques. Credit cards (especially Visa and MasterCard) are accepted by many hotels and restaurants but only by a few petrol stations, tavernas and shops. Bank opening hours are Mon–Thu 8am–2pm, Fri 8am–1.30pm.

NEWSPAPERS

Foreign newspapers can usually be bought on Corfu one day after they appear. The English language weekly *Athens News* and monthly *The Corfiot* are published locally. *Corfu Gazette* and *The Agiot* are two monthly electronic newsletters.

PHONE & MOBILE PHONE

With the exception of some emergency numbers, all Greek telephone numbers have ten digits. There are no area dialling codes. Greek mobile phone numbers always begin with "6".

Dialling codes: Greece 0030 followed by the telephone number. Code for Australia (0061), Canada (001), Ireland (00353), United Kingdom (0044), USA (001) followed by the area code without "0".

Mobile phone (called *kinitós*) reception is generally good except in some valleys. If you are based in the north of Corfu, make sure you do not make calls over an Albanian provider. Much like everywhere else in the world, you will be lucky to find a working phonebox. Should you stumble across one, you need to buy a phonecard (*statheró*) from a kiosk before trying to place a call.

PHOTOGRAPHY

Despite the fact that taking photos has become a regular feature in our daily lives, there are a few things to be aware of. Taking pictures of military areas is forbidden. In museums, there is often a fee if you want to film. You may also need permission and to pay a fee to take photos using a tripod or flash. Taking photographs is frowned upon in churches.

POST

There are post offices in Kérkyra and all major villages. It usually takes three to seven days for post to reach other European destinations. The large post offices always have a small selection of, often unusual, collectors' stamps. Post offices are usually open from Mon–Fri 7.30am–3pm.

PUBLIC HOLIDAYS

1 Jan	New Year's Day
6 Jan	Epiphany
Early March	Shrove Monday (start of Lent)
25 March	Annunciation Day
March/April	Good Friday; Easter Sunday

1 May	International Labour Day
21 May	Ionian Island Day
June	Whit Monday
15 Aug	Assumption Day
28 Oct	Ochi Day
25 / 26 Dec	Christmas

SHOPS

Most smaller shops are open Mon–Sat 8.30am–2pm and Tue, Thu, Fri from 6–9pm. Supermarkets and souvenir shops are generally open every day 9.30am–11pm.

SMOKING

Smoking is prohibited on all forms of public transport, in airport terminals, inside restaurants and tavernas, in offices and in the public areas of the hotels. However, these laws are only observed sporadically in restaurants and tavernas in the country.

TOILETS

Due to frequent problems with blocked pipes, used toilet paper should not be flushed in Corfu. Instead use the small bins next to the toilet. This can take some getting used to but is the rule across Corfu, no matter how luxurious your accommodation is.

TIPPING

Rules on tipping in Corfu are similar to across the rest of Europe (around 10%), but it is considered rude not to leave at least 50 cents. In restaurants, you leave the tip on the table when leaving.

WEATHER

High season
Low season

	JAN	FEB	MAR	APR	MAY	JUN	JUL	AUG	SEPT	OCT	NOV	DEC
Daytime temperatures (°C)	16°	16°	17°	20°	24°	28°	29°	29°	27°	24°	21°	17°
Night-time temperatures (°C)	9°	9°	10°	12°	15°	19°	21°	22°	19°	16°	14°	11°
☀ Hours of sunshine per day	3	5	6	8	10	12	13	12	10	6	6	4
🌧 Rainfall days per month	12	7	8	4	2	1	0	0	2	6	6	10
≈ Sea temperature (°C)	16	15	16	16	19	22	24	25	24	23	20	17

☀ Hours of sunshine per day   🌧 Rainfall days per month   ≈ Sea temperature (°C)

USEFUL WORDS & PHRASES

SMALLTALK

Yes/no/maybe	ne/ˈochi/ˈissos	Ναι/ Όχι/Ισως
Please/Thank you	parakaˈlo/efcharisˈto	Παρακαλώ/ Ευχαριστώ
Good morning/good evening/goodnight!	kalliˈmera/kalliˈspera/ kalliˈnichta!	Καλημέραμ/ Καλησπέρα!/ Καληνύχτα!
Hello/ goodbye (formal)/ goodbye (informal)	ˈya (su/sass)/aˈdio/ ya (su/sass)!	Γεία (σου/σας)!/ αντίο!/Γεία (σου/ σας)!
My name is …	me ˈlene …	Με λένεÖ …
What's your name?	poss sass ˈlene?	Πως σας λένε?
Excuse me/sorry	me sigˈchorite/ sigˈnomi	Με συγχωρείτε / Συγνώημ
Pardon?	oˈriste?	Ορίστε?
I (don't) like this	Afˈto (dhen) mu aˈressi	Αυτό (δεν) ουμ αρέσει

SYMBOLS

EATING & DRINKING

English	Pronunciation	Greek
Could you please book a table for tonight for four?	Klis'te mass parakal'lo 'enna tra'pezi ya a'popse ya 'tessera 'atoma	Κλείστε ασμ παρακαλώ ένα τραπέζι γιά απόψε γιά τέσσερα άτοαμ
The menu, please	tonn ka'taloggo parakal'lo	Τον κατάλογο παρακαλώ
Could I please have ... ?	tha 'ithella na 'echo ...?	Θα ήθελα να έχω ...?
More/less	pjo/li'gotäre	ρτιό/λιγότερο
with/without ice/ sparkling	me/cho'ris 'pa-go/ anthrakik'ko	εμ/χωρίς πάγο/ ανθρακικό
(un)safe drinking water	(mi) 'possimo nä'ro	(μη) Πόσιμο νερό
vegetarian/allergy	chorto'fagos/allerg'ia	Χορτοφάγος/ Αλλεργία
May I have the bill, please?	'thel'lo na pli'rosso parakal'lo	Θέλω να πληρώσω παρακαλώ

MISCELLANEOUS

English	Pronunciation	Greek
Where is ...?	pu tha vro ...?	Που θα βρω ...?
What time is it?	Ti 'ora 'ine?	Τι ώρα είναι?
How much does... cost ?	Posso 'kani ...?	Πόσο κάνει ...?
Where can I find internet access?	pu bor'ro na vro 'prosvassi sto indernett?	Που πορώμ να βρω πρόσβαση στο ίντερνετ?
pharmacy/ chemist	farma'kio/ ka'tastima	Φαρακείομ/ Κατάστηαμ καλλυντικών
fever/pain /diarrhoea/ nausea	piret'tos/'ponnos/ dhi'arria/ana'gula	Πυρετός/Πόνος/ Διάρροια/Αναγούλα
Help!/Watch out! Be Careful	Wo'ithia!/Prosso'chi!/ Prosso'chi!	Βοήθεια!/Προσοχή!/ Προσοχή!
Forbidden/banned	apa'goräfsi/ apago'räwäte	Απαγόρευση/ απαγορέυεται
0/1/2/3/4/5/6/7/8/9/ 10/100/1000	mi'dhen / 'enna / 'dhio / 'tria / 'tessera / 'pende /'eksi/ ef'ta / och'to / e'nea / dhekka / eka'to / 'chilia / 'dhekka chil'iades	ηδένμ/ένα/δύο/τρία/ τέσσερα/πέντε/έξι/ εφτά/οχτώ/ εννέα/ δέκα/εκατό/χίλια/ δέκα χιλιάδες

HOLIDAY VIBES

FOR RELAXATION AND CHILLING

FOR BOOKWORMS AND FILM BUFFS

📖 MY FAMILY AND OTHER ANIMALS
Gerald Durrell's humorous and much-loved description of his experiences on Corfu, where he spent his childhood in the 1930s.

📖 PROSPERO'S CELL: A GUIDE TO THE LANDSCAPE AND MANNERS OF THE ISLAND OF CORFU
Gerald's even more famous brother, Lawrence Durrell, captured the feeling of 1930s' Corfu in his works of literature.

🎥 FEDORA
Billy Wilder's bizarre story of a Hollywood star who also spent some time on Corfu; with Hildegard Knef and Mario Adorf in the main roles.

🎥 FOR YOUR EYES ONLY
The James Bond adventure story begins off the coast of Corfu, and parts of it were shot on the island in 1980.

A PLAYLIST FOR ALL TASTES

`0:58`

II ROTTING CHRIST
THEIR GREATEST SPELLS
This best-of is the perfect introduction to Greece's most famous Black Metal band.

▶ GIÓRGOS DALÁRAS
I MEGALÍTERES EPITÍHES TOU
A selection of hits from Greece's answer to Bruce Springsteen and one of the country's most famous artists.

▶ ÉLENA PAPARÍZOU
MY NUMBER ONE
The first time Greece won the Eurovision Song Contest was in 2005, and this (believe it or not) was the song that did it.

▶ VICKY LEANDROS SINGS MIKIS THEODORAKIS
Leandros was born on Corfu at Paleokastrítsa. She is a pop singer, but on this album she sings some of Greece's most famous composers' music.

Your holiday soundtrack can be found on Spotify under MARCO POLO Greece

Or scan this code with Spotify app

ONLINE

IN-CORFU.COM
Photos, ratings and articles about more than 100 beaches on the island.

CRUISETIMETABLES.COM
If you want to know the best time to visit some of the island's best sites, it is well worth knowing when cruise ships are harbouring around the coast ... so that you can avoid them. A quick glance at this website – especially before going into Corfu Town or visiting Achíllion and Paleokastrítsa – could be the difference between a nice day out or a day stuck in queues.

MARINE TRAFFIC
If you want to know what is going on around the island, this app allows you to see where the boats you can see from the coast are headed and where they have come from.

FLIGHTRADAR
If you get bored of looking out to sea, glance up to the sky ... which is every bit as busy. Flightradar app allows you to see where planes have set off from and where they are going. It can also be very useful if you want to know why your budget airline flight is so late!

TRAVEL PURSUIT

MARCO POLO'S HOLIDAY QUIZ

So you think you know what makes Corfu tick? Test your knowledge of the idiosyncrasies and eccentricities of the island and its people. You'll find the answers at the foot of the page, with more detailed explanations on pp18–23.

❶ Konstantinoúpolis means Constantine's City. It is still the Greek name for a modern city. But which one?
a) Canterbury
b) Istanbul
c) Rome

❷ Which late member of the British Royal Family was born on Corfu during the 20th century?
a) Princess Margaret
b) Prince Philip
c) The Queen Mother

❸ Sisi is the name of a European empress who owned a palace on Corfu. Which modern-day country did she rule?
a) Spain
b) Austria
c) Mexico

❹ What is the Greek name for the classic protest songs sung during the 1920s and 1930s?
a) Souvlakia
b) Rembetika
c) Tralalatika

Achillion

❺ What unusual gift can Greek Olympic medallists receive?
a) Gyms
b) Jet skis
c) Betting licences

❻ What is often found in sacks deposited under olive trees?
a) Animal dung
b) Domestic rubbish
c) Post rejected by the recipients

❼ Corfiots love their *paréas*, what are they referring to?
a) A special quilt used on the beach
b) A dinner party
c) A sword fight

❽ How do you spell the Greek word for a saint (using the Latin alphabet)?
a) Agios
b) Aghios
c) Ayios

❾ Arsenal and Man United are not the only clubs in Europe to wear red and white. Which Greek club has these colours?
a) AS Korfu
b) Olympiakós Piräus
c) Panthináikos Athen

❿ What does the Greek phrase "*ta léme*" mean?
a) Let's see
b) Sounds great
c) Fancy a beer?

⓫ How do Corfiots refer to the post-2008 financial crisis in Greece?
a) katástrophis
b) krísis
c) germanítis

INDEX

Acharávi 30, **66**, 69, 113, 121
Achíllion 11, 14, 56, **57**, 139, 141
Afiónas 18, **75**, 114
Agía Ekateríni **74**
Agías Efthímias, Kérkyra **48**, 119
Ágii Theodóri, Kérkyra 118
Ágios Geórgios North (Pagón) 8, 16,35, **75** 81, 115
Ágios Geórgios South (Argirádon) 16, 35, **92**, 95, 116
Ágios Górdis 16, **86**, 116
Ágios Nikólaos Beach 104
Ágios Nikólas Gate, Kérkyra 44
Ágios Spirídonas Beach 69, 74, 121
Ágios Spirídonas Church, Kérkyra **42**,
Ágios Stéfanos 16, **75**,114
Ágios Stéfanos Avliotón 31
Ágios Stéfanos Siniés **65**, 122
Agní **65**
Almirós Beach 69
Alonáki 11, **93**, 95, 116
Análipsi 119
Anemómilos, Kérkyra 120
Angelókastro 80, **81**, 115
Áno Korakiána 33, **105**, 120
Archaeological Museum, Kérkyra 47, 133
Arillás **75**, 114, 131
Astrakéri 72
Avláki Beach 63, 64
Batería Beach 63, 64, 122
Bénitses 131
Boúkari **90**, 117
British Cemetery, Kérkyra 47
Butrint, Albanien 126

Byzantine Museum, Kérkyra 45, 133
Cambiéllo, Kérkyra 44, 45
Canal d'Amour 70,71, 113
Cape Akrotíri Agías Ekaterínis 34
Cape Akrotíri Arkoúdia 34
Cape Drástis 16, **71**, 113
Cemetery Church, Kérkyra 117
Chlómos 90
Corfu Town (Kérkyra) 10, 15, 17, 38, 117, 128, 129, 130, 131, 132, 134
Corfu Trail 34
Dafníla 34, **102**
Dassiá 33, 35, **102**
Doric Temple, Kérkyra 48, 119
Érmones 33, 35, **110**
Esplanade, Kérkyra 10, 42, 45, 47, 54
Faliráki, Kérkyra 44
Faliráki Beach 54
Folklore Museum, Sinarádes 111, 116
Gardíki **94**, 116
Gialiskári Beach 65
Glifáda 16, **107**
Glifáda Beach 109, 131
Gouviá 32, 33, **100**,123
Ípsos 105
Kaiser's Throne **107**, 116
Kalámi **66**, 122
Kamináki Beach 66
Kanóni, Kérkyra 10, 49, 55
Kassiopi **62**, 122, 131
Kávos 16, **95**
Kérkyra (Corfu Town) 10, 15, 17, **38**, 128, 129, 130, 131, 134
Komméno 104
Kontokáli 35, **100**, 101
Kouloúra **66**, 122
Lake Koríssion **92**, 116
Lákones 30, 77, **80**, 115
Lefkími 21, **94**, 116
Makrádes 30, **81**, 115

Messongí **88**, 117, 131
Mirtiótissa 107, **108**, 109
Mon Repos, Kérkyra **48**, 55, 119
Moní Myrtidión 108
Moraítika 88, 117
Néa Períthia 73
New Fortress (Néo Froúrio), Kérkyra 44, 55
Nímfes 72
Nissáki 122
Nótos Beach 91
Old Fortress, Kérkyra **42**, 43, 44, 48, 51, 131
Old Palace, Kérkyra 47
Pági 115
Palaiópolis Basilica, Kérkyra **48**, 119
Paleokastrítsa 16, 33, 34, 35, **77**, 115,125, 131
Paleokastrítsa Monastery 78
Paleó Períthia **73**, 121, 132
Panagía Antivuniótissa, Kérkyra 45
Panagía Kassiópitra, Kassiópi 63
Panagía Mirtiótissa 108
Panagía Theotóku tis Paleokastrítsas 78
Pantokrátor **72**, 73, 113,120
Paramónas **88**, 116
Páxos 32
Pélekas 16, **107**, 116, 130, 132
Pélekas Beach 109
Pendáti **87**, 116
Perouládes **70**, 113
Petríti **91**, 117
Pirgí 105
Pontikoníssi, Kérkyra 49
Róda **66**, 68, 113
Rópa Valley 33, 108, **110**, 115
Sidári **71**, 113
Sinarádes **111**, 116
Sokráki **106**, 120
Spartílas 113
Strinílas 30, **72**, 120

Temple of Artemis, Kérkyra 118

Temple of Kardáki, Kérkyra 119

Venetian Shipyard, Gouviá 100

Vlachérna, Kérkyra **49**, 102

Vídos, Kérkyra 49

WE WANT TO HEAR FROM YOU!

Did you have a great holiday? Is there something on your mind? Whatever it is, let us know! Whether you want to praise the guide, alert us to errors or give us a personal tip – MARCO POLO would be pleased to hear from you.

We do everything we can to provide the very latest information for your trip. Nevertheless, despite all of our authors' thorough research, errors can creep in. MARCO POLO does not accept any liability for this. Please contact us by e-mail.

e-mail: sales@heartwoodpublishing.co.uk

Picture credits
Cover: Paleokastritsa Bay (istock/ Elenasfotos)
Photographs: AWL Images: N. Farrin (140/141); AWL Images/Danita Delimont Stock (back flap); K. Bötig (91, 143); Getty Images: L. Delderfield (11), P. Kazmierczak (82/83), A. Spatari (19), van den Bergh (49); M. Hackenberg (46, 80); huber-images: F. Cogoli (138/139), B. Cossa (104), D. Erbetta (9, 24/25, 110), O. Fantuz (76/77, 127), P. Panayiotou (35), A. Pavan (108), R. Schmid (14/15, 26/27, 54, 56, 58/59, 63, 64, 69, 122/123), G. Simeone (6/7); Laif: T. Linkel (28), T. & B. Morandi (38/39), Trummer (78), R. Wichert (115); Laif/ robertharding: N. Farrin (50); E. Laue (103); Look: S. Dürichen (10); mauritius images/Alamy: 3dool3 (44), D. M. Balate (70/71), R. Dyke (12/13), O. Gajewska (101), J. Gravell (124), B. Kean (118/119), A. Mroszczyk (30/31), R. Musser (32/33), G. Rooney (31, 73), A. Varanishcha (2/3, 74), D. Vlassis (92/93, 131), A. Zelenov (outer front flap, inner front flap/1); mauritius images/Alamy/Alltravel (87, 112/113); mauritius images/Alamy/Imageimage (128/129); mauritius images/Cultura (94); mauritius images/ Foodanddrinkphotos (27); mauritius images/image-broker (96/97), N. Probst (8, 43); mauritius images/ robertharding: T. Graham (20); mauritius images/ Westend61: E. Birk (23); T. Stankiewicz (52, 107); Visum/MeystPhoto.com: F. Meyst (34)

4th Edition – fully revised and updated 2022
Worldwide Distribution: Heartwood Publishing Ltd, Bath, United Kingdom
www.heartwoodpublishing.co.uk

© MAIRDUMONT GmbH & Co. KG, Ostfildern
Author: Klaus Bötig; **editor:** Marlis von Hessert-Fraatz
Picture editor: Veronika Plajer
Cartography: © MAIRDUMONT, Ostfildern (pp. 36-37, 114, 119, 121, 124, 126, back cover, pull-out map); © MAIRDUMONT, Ostfildern, using map data from OpenStreetMap, Lizenz CC-BY-SA 2.0 (pp. 40-41, 60-61, 66, 84-85, 89, 98-99).
Cover design and pull-out map cover design: bilekjaeger_Kreativagentur mit Zukunftswerkstatt, Stuttgart; **page designs:** Langenstein Communication GmbH, Ludwigsburg
Text on the back flap: Lucia Rojas

Heartwood Publishing credits:
Translated from the German by John Owen, Robert McInnis and Susan Jones
Editors: Kate Michell and Sophie Blacksell Jones
Prepress: Summerlane Books, Bath
Printed in India

MARCO POLO AUTHOR
KLAUS BÖTIG
Author of the most widely read guidebooks in Germany, Klaus Bötig is happy to spend his time travelling from place to place. He considers it his duty to taste every Corfiot speciality on behalf of his readers, and treasures the memory of this magical island as a source of consolation when he's stuck at his desk on a soggy day in his native Bremen.

DOS & DON'TS!

HOW TO AVOID SLIP-UPS AND BLUNDERS

DON'T ASK ABOUT THE COMPETITION

If you go into a taverna and ask about a rival establishment, you may be told that it doesn't exist, that the landlord has died or the police have closed it down.

DON'T ACT LIKE THE PAPARAZZI

Many Corfiots like to be photographed if they are nicely dressed for a special occasion, but always seek permission first. Before you release the shutter, smile at the person you want to photograph and wait for his or her agreement.

DON'T BE BROWBEATEN

Travel reps live from commissions. Most give honest information – but there are some who try to make their guests feel uncertain so that they will book their cars through them or take part in organised excursions instead of travelling by bus or taxi. Corfu is a safe island and there is no reason not to travel independently.

DON'T FORGET YOUR HIKING SHOES

Sandals are not even suitable for short hikes; you should at least wear sturdy trainers. The paths are often stony and slippery. And there are snakes – only a few and they are timid, but you never know. Long trousers will protect you from thorns.

DON'T BE SHOCKED BY THE PRICE OF FISH

Fresh fish has been extremely expensive in some Greek restaurants and tavernas for years. It is often sold by weight. You should ask how much a kilogram costs and be there when it is weighed so that you don't have any unpleasant surprises.